ROUGH RUDE MEN

A Deal Lugger making for the Goodwin Sands. Edwin Weedon 1872.

ROUGH RUDE MEN

A History of Old-Time Kentish Smuggling

John Douch

'Nor must we forget that those rough, rude men who ran backwards and forwards across the English Channel in cutters, yawls, luggers and sometimes open boats, stiffened with a rich ballast of tea, tobacco and brandy, were some of the finest seamen in the world . . . sturdy and strong of body, courageous and enterprising of nature.'

E. K. Chatterton, *King's Cutters and Smugglers.* 1912

Crabwell Publications/Buckland Publications Ltd.
2 The Ridgeway, River, Dover.

To Ralph Finn

The author is pleased to state that a share of the proceeds from this book is promised to the Royal National Lifeboat Institution whose lifeboat *Rotary Service* is stationed at his home town of Dover.

Published jointly by Crabwell Publications
and Buckland Publications Ltd., 1985.

ISBN 0 906124 07 7

Printed in England by Buckland Press Ltd., Barwick Road, Dover
and 125 High Holborn, London WC1

CONTENTS

John Mills alias *Smoaker*, & *Rich.ᵈ Rowland* alias
Robb, Whipping *Rich.ᵈ Hawkins*, to Death, at y̓ Dog & Par
tridge on *Slendon Common*; & *Jeremiah Curtis*, & *Tho.ˢ Winter*
alias *Coachman*, Standing by aiding & abetting y̓ Murder
of the said *Rich.ᵈ Hawkins*.

The Gruesome Hawkhurst Gang.   (Old print)

ILLUSTRATIONS

BIBLIOGRAPHY AND MAIN SOURCES

Books

Anon. *Sussex Smugglers* 1749
Arnold-Foster, D. *At War with the Smugglers* 1936
Atton, H. and Holland, H. H. *The King's Customs* 1910
Brent, C. E. (compiler) *Smuggling through Sussex* 1977
Carson, E. *The Ancient and Rightful Customs* 1972
Chatterton, E. K. *King's Cutters and Smugglers* 1912
Clark, K. M. *Smuggling in Rye and District* 1977
Cooper, W. *Smuggling in Sussex* 1858
Douch, J. A. *Smuggling — The Wicked Trade* 1980
Farjeon, J. J. *The Compleat Smuggler* 1938
Glascock, W. N. *Naval Sketch Book* (series 1) 1832
Harvey, W. *Whitstable and the French Prisoners of War* 1971
Hoon, E. *The Origin of the English Customs System (1696-1786)* 1968
James, G. P. R. *The Smuggler* 1845
Lapthorne, W. H. *Smugglers' Broadstairs* 1970
Leitch, M. *The Romance of Sail* 1975
Lloyd, C. *Captain Marryat and the Old Navy* 1938
Martin, N. *Search and Rescue* 1974
Masefield, J. *Sea Life in Nelson's Time* 1905
'Old Folkestone Free-trader, An' *Smugglers and Smuggling Days* 1883
Scarlett, B. *Shipminder* 1971
Smith, G. *Something to Declare* 1980
Spence, K. *The Companion Guide to Kent and Sussex* 1973
Teignmouth, Lord and Harper, C. G. *The Smugglers* 1923
Webb, W. *Coastguard!* 1976
Western, J. R. *The English Militia in the 18th Century* 1970
Williams, N. *Contraband Cargoes* 1959
Winslow, C. Section in *Albion's Fatal Tree* 1975

Articles and Papers

Askew, M. *They all want putting down (Coast and Country* IX no. 4)

Collier, J. *Papers relating to Custom House Matters 1713-50* ed. Sayer C. L. (deposited at East Sussex Record Office, Lewes)

Finn, J. *A Manuscript Journal of his Life* transcribed and set down by his son Edward ca 1850 (unpublished)

Lloyd, C. *The Blockade of the Smugglers (History Today* XXVII no 12)

Muskett, P. *Military Operations against Smuggling in Kent and Sussex 1698-1750 (Journal for the Society of Army Historical Research* LII)

Shanes E. *Turner's Secret* 1981

Personal Communications

Mrs J. Blackman, Chichester   L. M. Chowns, Shadoxhurst

L. W. Cozens, Deal   R. Finn, Ramsgate

W. H. Lapthorne, Broadstairs   Mrs J. Lodey, East Dereham

R. H. Perks, Faversham   L. Pierce, Goudhurst

P. Muskett, Ely   R. C. Sayer, Great Walsingham

The Honorary Secretaries of:

Ashford Archaeological and Historical Society

Biddenden Local History Society

Brenchley Historical Society

Deal, Walmer and District History Society

The Eltham Society

The Faversham Society

Gravesend Historical Society

Ightham and District Historical Society

Lewisham Local History Society

Meopham Historical Society

Otford and District Historical Society

Sandwich Local History Society

Sheppey Local History Society

The Sittingbourne Society

Introduction

Kent makes good claim to the best recorded, the most eventful and possibly the bloodiest smuggling history of any county in the kingdom; it is against this undeniably brutal but not, I think, completely repulsive background that I have displayed the Kentish fair-trader (as he would have called himself) at work. "Woe to the author who is always wanting to instruct; the secret of boring is that of saying everything"—it is with Voltaire's warning in mind that I have as far as possible eschewed repetition of many incidents recounted in my previous book (which dealt exclusively with Romney Marsh) or, where this has been unavoidable, I have attempted to view them differently. I have similarly not lingered long over those good old favourites which now seem to be wearing rather threadbare—the gruesome Hawkhurst characters, the battle of Goudhurst, the terrible fate of Customs Officer Galley and the informer Chater the cobbler—all have earned their rightful niches in Kent's smuggling lore and all have been gone over time and again in the past hundred years or so. Here, therefore, I merely mention them so that the picture, as far as possible, shall be complete (although, for obvious reasons, a 'complete' smuggling history of any place, however small, is an impossibility; the amount and value of the successfully 'run' contraband can never be estimated and all that can be said is that, like the tip of the proverbial iceberg, the amount recovered was proportionally minute).

What then is left to be told? After having related the Trade's development from its early 'owling' origins to its zenith and ultimate destruction some two centuries later, and after having given some account of the counter-measures it provoked — an understanding of these being essential to appreciate how the smugglers worked — it would seem that I have somehow produced a guide to the everyday 'nuts and bolts' of Kentish fair-trading.

Many places of particular smuggling interest are still identifiable; wherever possible I have illustrated them, some as they were and some as they are. I gratefully acknowledge the kind help and encouragement given by Eddie Clapson, Ralph Finn, Harold Gough, Wallace Harvey, Bill Lapthorne and Paul Muskett. Finally, I am happy to record the considerable response from the many local history groups throughout the county who kindly answered my request for hitherto unpublished information from their respective areas; my one regret is that lack of space alone precludes individual mention of each and every Kentish village which still remembers with a little quiet pride the association it once had with its own locally produced Rough, Rude Men.

Sources of Illustrations

The author's original photographs are on pages 20 (bottom), 26, 28 (top), 33 (top), 46, 47, 48, 49, 50, 51, 54, 55, 95, 102, 110, 111, 121, 125 (top) and 142.

The following were supplied by and are reproduced by kind permission of: Dover Library: 18 (top), 80, 129, 136; Gravesend Historical Society: 22, 33 (bottom); Mr. W. Harvey: 114; Herne Bay Records Society: 72, 127, 141; Mr W. Lapthorne (Broadstairs Local Historian and Recorder of the Isle of Thanet Archaeological Trust): 2, 23, 35, 74, 76, 77, 82 (bottom), 84 (bottom), 123, 145.

Of the remainder, some are acknowledged within the text; of the others, the author has been unable to trace the copyright holders, if any. He accordingly expresses regret for any inadvertent omission of due attribution and trusts that this explanation will be accepted as an apology for the same.

Owlers, Caterpillars or Gentlemen?

Smuggling has a long history—even ancient Carthage had problems with Customs evasions—but our story starts in mediaeval Kent with the Owlers, stout if not honest fellows who made a good living by illegally shipping wool from Kent to the Continent. There is no certain answer as to why they were so called; possibly they used the owl's cry as a signal or maybe the word is a transposition of 'wooller' or, perhaps, they preferred to work by night . . .

Officially, smugglers were not popular with the Establishment of their day, and yet one 17th century writer complained bitterly that "these caterpillars" continually escaped their just deserts and lawful punishments, "such favour have they in the courts of justice".

'Gentlemen', a euphemism applied to the practitioners of Defoe's "wicked trade from Romney Marsh" is another term whose exact origin is long forgotten. It was Rudyard Kipling, however, who fixed it for all time in the public imagination in his *Smuggler's Song*, underlining the undoubted fact that smugglers, like gentlemen, were by no means confined to a single social class:

> Brandy for the Parson, 'baccy for the clerk;
> Laces for a lady, letters for a spy;
> And watch the wall, my darling,
> While the Gentlemen go by . . .

An early Ordnance Survey map of Kent (1807) with later additions e.g. railways.

The Home of the Kentish Smuggler

Of all counties the most favoured by nature and by art for the very pleasant and exciting sport of smuggling was Kent.

G. P. R. James, a writer now practically forgotten, achieved considerable success in his day with a three-volume blockbuster of a novel *The Smuggler* published in 1845. Whatever reservations today's reader may have about his style, there can be little doubt that James knew his subject and his Kent very well indeed and it is from his work (ruthlessly edited of its flowery digressions) that one quickly and easily gains an impression of what the terrain must have been like in the 18th century, in which period the novel is set:

'A long range of hills, varying greatly in height and steepness, runs nearly down the centre of the county, throwing out spurs and buttresses in different directions, sometimes leaving broad and beautiful valleys between. The origin of this range is the great Surrey chain of hills (with in many places a separation through which the Medway, the Stour and several smaller rivers flow into the Thames or on to the sea). The general connection, however, is sufficiently marked and from Dover and Folkestone, by Lenham, Chart, Maidstone and Westerham on the one side and Barham, Harbledown and Rochester in the other, the road runs generally over a long line of elevated ground, only dipping down here and there to visit some town or city of importance which

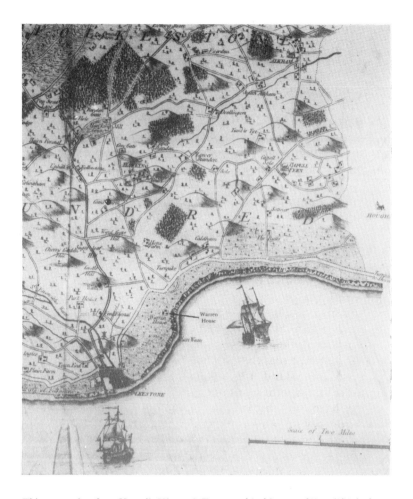

This map, taken from Hasted's *History & Topographical Survey of Kent* (1795), shows Warren House, 'the most convenient place in England for communicating with France', long since demolished. In 1698, it was acquired by the government and troops were stationed there to deal with the smugglers but they still continued to use its grounds; one night, silks and lace value £3,000 were hidden there. Well over a century ago an inn and, later, a tea-garden occupied the site. These too have disappeared, giving way to caravans, it is now called 'Little Switzerland'.

has nested itself in one of the lateral valleys or strayed out onto the plain. On the northern side of the county, a considerable extent of the flat ground extends along the bank and the estuary of the Thames from Greenwich to Sandwich and Deal. On the southern side, a still wider extent lies between the high land and the borders of Sussex. This plain or valley terminates at the sea by the renowned flat of Romney Marsh. Farther up, somewhat narrowing as it goes, it becomes the Weald of Kent, comprising some very rich land and a number of small villages with one or two towns of no great importance. The Weald is bordered all along by the hilly range already mentioned, the high road from London pursues its way up and down hill by Lenham and Charing and thence to Ashford and on to Folkestone. Thus, a great part of the Weald was totally untravelled and I have myself seen the whole population of a village of considerable size, which now hears almost hourly the panting and screaming steam-engine whirling by, turn out to behold the wonderful phenomenon of a coach-and-four, the first that was ever beheld in the place. Close to the sea, the hills are bare enough but at no great distance inland they become rich in wood and the Weald, whether arable or pasture, hop-garden or orchard, is divided into small fields by numerous hedgerows of fine trees and so diversified by patches of woodland that, seen at a distance up a hill, it assumes in the leafy season the look of a forest partially cleared . . . '

It was at about this time that a captain of Dragoons on anti-smuggling patrol in the district reported to his general:

'If you intend that we should go to Maidstone or Tunbridge or Grinsted, it would be very proper to make the War Office send us a discretionary route, because they know nothing at all of the country, nor of the roads, that are worse than can be imagined by people that have not seen them . . . '

Dover Customs House by J. Gendall 1820.

Ramsgate Harbour 1805.

18

The same officer refers to an additional peril attributed to smugglers:

'The Mange or General Leprosie spreads every Day more & more about the Country—all the Farriers saye it and the Farmers loose many Horses . . . this Distemper by all accts seizes ye Horses very suddenly, they are covered all over with a scurf an inch thick, & they dye in a few Days. The men who follow them in ye Roads without Boots catch it; the known & common remedies agst ye Mange don't cure them. It is the Smugglers' Horses that give it to the Others . . . this may spread all along ye Sea Coast, & perhaps all over ye Country, because it is ye Smugglers' Horses that have it most . . .'

Communications throughout the country, especially in the Weald, were indeed truly execrable. The few turnpike roads apart, in many places the most reliable means of transport was either on horseback or in the ox-cart—a mode which, slow but sure, persisted in some localities (certainly on Romney Marsh) until the end of the 19th century. Daniel Defoe (*A Tour through England and Wales* 1724) was impressed by the practice:

'Here I had a sight which indeed I never saw in any other part of England: namely, that going to church at a country village, not far from Lewes, I saw an ancient lady, and a lady of very good quality, I assure you, drawn to church in her coach with six oxen; nor was it done in frolic or humour, but sheer necessity, the way being so stiff and deep that no horses could go in it.'

Despite James's eulogies, the fact must be faced that parts of Kent in those days were, to put it mildly, not very nice places in which to live. The grisly reputation of Romney Marsh—'Evil in Winter, grievous in Summer and never good'—was second only to that of the Hoo peninsula between the estuaries of the Thames and the Medway: 'A most beastly place . . . mist, swamp and work; work, swamp, mist and mudbank.' (Dickens' *Great Expectations*.) This was without

'Not even the church was exempted . . .' *Minster in Thanet* 1832 'Great pews, fiddlers and smugglers had it pretty much their own way here for many a year. The smugglers felt so comfortable that they actually took out stones from the wall as a safe storehouse for their kegs and the strong smell of contraband liquor often regaled the singers in the gallery above.' (From a paper read by the Vicar, the Revd F. Gell, at a parish meeting 22nd July 1879).

St George's, Ivychurch, Romney Marsh.
Also used as a smuggler's storehouse.

doubt the dreariest and the least hospitable region of the whole county; Samuel Ireland, the Kent historian writing in 1830, supports Dickens' view: 'There is scarcely a gentleman's house or even a clergyman living there, in consequence of the depth of the soil, the dirtiness of the roads, and the unwholesome air issuing from its neigbouring marshes . . .'

For all these drawbacks—and drawbacks they hardly were from a smuggling point of view—nature more than compensated by endowing Kent with a superabundance of excellent landing-places finely secluded and far enough removed from the eye of officialdom and yet reasonably near both to the source of contraband and to the lucrative London market. Each part of the coast had its differing potentialities and cargoes could be unloaded almost anywhere—upon the shingly wastes of Dungeness, beneath the familiar towering white cliffs of Dover (within rowing distance of Calais), on to the stony beach of 'that sad smuggling town of Deal'; up and around the North Foreland and away on past the fishing villages of Ramsgate, Broadstairs and Margate (all soon destined to burgeon with the advent of the railway into genteel watering-places for the jaded Londoner in search of sea breezes). Here it was that one might have noticed 'the many private gates cut down through the cliffs that strike up the fields directly to some of the villages or great farm-houses, not a mile from the sea.' Onward then, on into the misty ague-ridden fastnesses of the Swale and the estuaries of the Medway and the Thames, up even into the Port of London itself—everywhere beaches, creeks, inlets and havens galore where a small craft cunningly handled might nose her way in unseen to unload, then with a fair wind slip off still unobserved. It was not only the seaboard which favoured the Kentish smuggler; inland were dense woodland tracts—remnants of the forest of Anderida—and country estates with vast areas of parkland traversable only on foot or horseback, and then often with some difficulty. The free-traders knew, and were able to circumnavigate, most natural obstacles; the entire Weald of

21

The Bawley Bay, Gravesend, 1870.
These vessels were not above carrying a little contraband.

Kent was criss-crossed by the prehistoric 'hollow ways' once used by the Phoenician traders but by then reduced to overgrown sunken tracks known only to deer, foxes, poachers, smugglers and the like:

> 'Not a park, not a wood, not a barn but did not at some period afford the smugglers a refuge when pursued or become a repository for their commodities . . . many a man on visiting his stable or cart-shed early in the morning found it tenanted by anything but horses and wagons. The churchyards were frequently crowded at night by other spirits than those of the dead and not even the church was exempted from these visitations.'

James Finn, one-time parish clerk and village schoolmaster of Mersham, a village just north of the Romney Marsh, kept a journal in which he describes the physical attributes and the activities of some of his fellow villagers. In his boyhood in the 1780s it was nothing for him to meet up with large smuggling gangs out and about their business in broad daylight; once, he came upon a string of eighty horses hauling wagons full of contraband on their way to London with an escort of 'hefty ill-looking ruffians who ignored everybody they met . . . thankfully, such sights are becoming rarer and rarer in these more enlightened days.'

A view showing the King's Gate from the landward side in 1816.   (Old print)

How the Customs evolved

The smuggler would have been in every respect an excellent citizen had not the laws of his country made that a crime which nature never meant to be so.

(Adam Smith, *The Wealth of Nations*, 1776)

To understand how the free or fair trader (he never looked upon himself as a smuggler) operated, one must appreciate in outline the development and the organisation of the system against which he pitted his not inconsiderable wits. First and foremost, the duty of the Customs official, as he saw it, was to examine commodities, imported and exported, with a view to collecting the lawful duty payable thereon; pursuit of the lawbreaker was a separate task which in the earlier days fell to private individuals armed with a royal warrant endowing them with special powers of arrest. Such a man was William Carter, a clothier, who in 1671 published his pamphlet against owling declaring that 'the misery of England is the great quantity of wool stolen out of the Country.' Endowed with a lion's share of courage, motivated by an amalgam of private interest and public concern, he pursued (and was often pursued by) owlers the length and breath of Romney Marsh and beyond. For more than a quarter of a century he brought fruitless prosecution after prosecution against them, becoming convinced that the Traders had friends in high places. In 1690, he pleaded for a small frigate to patrol between Dover and Beachy Head; his request was refused on grounds of economy. Six years later he asked again with no better success;

he died fighting to the end, complaining bitterly of the slackness and the corruption which surrounded him and of the meanness of the few rewards which had come to him.

Soon after, however, things did start to move. The Government assumed responsibility for chasing the smugglers with the foundation of the Land and Water Guards (see later section).

Apart from the export tax on wool, the early Customs were also soon to be involved in import duties. These were first imposed on wine with the other main commodities of tea, tobacco, spirits, lace and silk (along with the more exotic items such as elephant's teeth and vulture's feathers) being added from time to time over the ensuing centuries. Since the Conquest, wine had been shipped over from France in ever increasing amounts. The standard beverage of the nobility, it was normally transported in barrels or 'tuns'; hence the carrying capacity or 'tonnage' of a ship to this day. The Crown, by ancient privilege, claimed one barrel out of every twenty unloaded, one being taken from before the mast and one from behind (a precaution to ensure that the king was not fobbed off with an inferior vintage handily positioned) under the supervision of a royal household official, the Bouteilleur or King's Butler, who deputed agents at certain designated ports, one of which was Sandwich, to collect this most important part of the king's income. With the Customs firmly established by 1203, it was centralised with Collectors stationed at many ports including Dover and Sandwich. Yet more revision followed with a new scheme — the Nova Customa — being introduced in 1275; by this time three important roles had emerged — the Searcher who inspected the goods, the Collector or Customer who calculated and collected the amounts due and the Controller who was in general overall supervision. Thus emerged the tripartite system which forms the basis of the Customs organisation today. Clearly, the system was not foolproof and the officials themselves not always above reproach; an instance from Tudor Faversham concerns the

Mayor who, with orders to arrest thirteen fellow citizens on charges regarding illegal brewing was unable to comply as not one of the suspects, including the Searcher himself, was to be found.

Many persons of note served the Customs in their time and Kent bred the most famous of them all, Geoffrey Chaucer (1340-1400), although there is some doubt as to his exact birthplace. With a family tradition of Customs service behind him, at 34 Chaucer was appointed Controller of exported wool, fells and leather at the Port of London. Eight years later saw him Controller of Petty Customs there, but it seems that he was not over-zealous in the conduct of his duties and paid a deputy to act for him. In 1386 his patron died and so Chaucer lost his appointment but Customs' loss was to prove posterity's gain for he was thus enabled to devote his whole life to writing. In his *Canterbury Tales*, Chaucer displays plenty of human foibles although he makes only two references to possible illicit trading by the Pilgrims; perhaps he felt it politic to be

The Old Customs House, Sandwich.

Geoffrey Chaucer, an early Customs officer.

discreet. He hints that the Shipman (sea-captain) may have dabbled in clandestine wine trading: 'Many a draught of vintage, red and yellow, he'd drawn at Bordeaux . . . the nicer rules of conscience he ignored.' The ultra-respectable Merchant was up to his neck in shady financial transactions in which wool must have played its part: 'He was expert at currency exchange, this estimable Merchant so had set his wits to work, none knew he was in debt, he was so stately in negotiation, loan, bargain and commercial obligation.'*

Canterbury Tales Chaucer ed. N. Coghill 1951

(Right) One of the three Smythe family tombs (they are all similar) in Ashford (Kent) Parish Church.

(Below) Westenhanger House, Kent The family home of Sir Thomas Smythe (see p.29) who, besides organising Queen Elizabeth's finances, had considerable interest in banking and Cornish mining of lead, tin, copper and silver. He helped finance Raleigh's exploration of the New World; for his services he was granted the Manors of Easternhanger and Westernhanger, near Folkestone, by the Queen in 1585 but was later to fall from favour when he found difficulty in finding the rent. (Legend has it that the Fair Rosamund, once mistress of Henry II, was imprisoned here.) (Old print)

Over one period, the Crown was not directly involved in the collection of the duties. Instead, a system of 'Customs farming' was followed whereby revenues were leased or 'farmed out' to the private individual in exchange for fixed payments to the Crown, the 'farmer' being left to collect the dues as best he could. This system reached its peak in Elizabethan times, with Sir Thomas ('Mr Customer') Smythe satisfactorily demonstrating to the Queen how the system could be made to work to her advantage and thus, so it was hoped, to the benefit of the whole nation.

By 1671, world-wide trade was expanding so rapidly that things got out of hand. A Royal Commission (which included the property developer Sir George Downing after whom the street is named) recommended fundamental changes; acting on its recommendations the Government once again took full control of the Customs. Every main port was allotted its own Controller, Searcher and Collector, along with a host of lesser mortals to do the more mundane practical tasks. There were tide waiters to board incoming vessels to check the cargo and also to carry out a most important secondary duty of enforcing the health regulations:

> 'The control of quarantine was firmly placed on the Customs service. In 1720 there was a serious outbreak of plague on the Continent and as a result more stringent regulations were introduced. Masters of vessels were compelled to bring their ships to approved boarding stations and to make a health declaration on oath. The Customs officer handed to the master at the end of a boat-hook a bible enclosed in an iron cover; after the declaration had been made, the 'Quarantine or Plague Bible' was dragged through the sea water in order to cleanse it.' (*Something to Declare*, G. Smith, 1980.)

This done, the tide waiter guided the vessel to her unloading berth where land waiters took over to re-check the cargo as it was taken off. Besides these two posts, king's waiters, preferential tide waiters, glutmen, piazzamen and many

29

another equally picturesquely titled positions were created to whom nominal salaries only were paid, it being assumed, perhaps not without reason, that a good living was to be made from the standard fees charged plus, one may guess, a modicum of sweeteners. Nepotism was indeed rife: 'When anyone fails in business, or a gentleman wants to part with an old servant, interest is made to get them into Customs as into a hospital.' A post advertised for a London landing waiter attracted five hundred applicants, each one the nominee of a person of influence.

'Away, away went the fleet dapple-grey'. (see p.131)

The Three Ages of Smuggling

Kent's story falls neatly into three chronological divisions, although there is naturally some inevitable overlapping. First was the age of the owler; his importance declined with the fall of the wool trade. As home weaving became established, there was a concurrent upsurge of trade with the New World, with Africa and with India, sometimes direct and sometimes through Europe. Coupled with the expansion of world trade came the dramatic increase in export taxation brought about by the need to finance wars both in Europe and in North America. So dawned the so-called Golden Epoch of smuggling with attention focused primarily on tea, tobacco, spirits and, to a lesser extent, silk and lace. With Napoleon's final defeat came a marked increase in both activity and violence by the gangs; well might it have been termed the Bloody End for indeed so it proved for many a colourful old-timer.

Owling Days

> Though Jason's fleece was famed of old*
> The British wool is growing gold.
> No mines can more of wealth supply,
> It keeps the peasant from the cold
> And takes for Kings the Tyrian dye**
>
> (John Dryden 1631-1700)

*Jason was the leader of a band of ancient Greek heroes. One of their tasks was to capture a golden fleece hanging in a tree guarded by a dragon.
**A purple dye reserved for royalty alone.

31

The poet was no doubt aware, although he fails to mention the fact, that the profits from owling kept many a Kentish farmer and landowner in degrees of comfort varying from affluence to downright opulence. Men of substance, so it was said, carried on their owling in a civilised fashion and it was only when a lower class of smuggler came to predominate in that upstart form of import smuggling that the Trade acquired a bad name; it has to be said, however, that there were plenty of skirmishes between the law and the owlers, especially on Romney Marsh. English wool, the best in the world, was highly sought after by the continental weavers. Ironically, although our sheep produced the top quality raw material, we lacked the weaving expertise and this was one reason why, in an effort to establish a home industry, the export of wool was for a time banned completely and skilled workers were invited to come over from the Netherlands to settle here, which they did, as the weavers' houses in various parts of the Weald bear witness to this very day.

Despite all attempts to exterminate him, the owler flourished. The introduction of the death penalty for wool smuggling (1662) appears merely to have stiffened his resolve and encouraged a wider use of firearms; in 1669 the Dover Customs officials appeared in the House of Lords, testifying that the owlers' strength was increasing and calling for military intervention; the forlorn hope was expressed that troops might be stationed in every village on the Kent coast. By the close of the century, wool smuggling reached its peak with Captain Henry Baker, Surveyor General of the Kent Riding Officers reporting that within a few weeks of 25th April 1699, 160,000 sheep would have been shorn on Romney Marsh, the total yield amounting to 3,000 wool-packs 'the greatest part of whereof will be immediately sent off hot into France—it being so designed, and provisions in a great measure already being made for that purpose.' Following a special enquiry, at long last eight Riding Officers were sanctioned for Kent, two to be stationed in each of the four

The George Inn, Lydd.
A notorious smuggling retreat (see
p.34) with Lydd Church ('the
Cathedral of the Marsh') in the
background. Many of the Trade are
buried here.

The Three Daws, Gravesend.   Another well known smuggling rendezvous.

most notorious smuggling centres, viz: Folkestone, Hythe, Lydd and New Romney ('where every house is an owler's').

It was at about this time, or perhaps a little earlier, that the owlers diversified and turned their attention to the import trade. One Hunt, reputedly a Jacobite, kept open house in the Marsh for 'men of high consideration — earls, knights, barons and doctors of divinity'. Were they the 'Gentlemen' of whom Kipling was to write some two hundred years later? Certainly, many of the items he lists in his 'Smuggler's Song' appear in an account of the commodities that passed through Hunt's hands — Lyons silk, Valenciennes lace (enough in one consignment alone to load thirty pack-horses) and the famous 'letters for a spy', there being a regular postal service by sea and land from London to the Court in exile at St Germaine as related by Macaulay in his *History of England*.

Even in times of war, the Kentish smugglers maintained their contacts across the Channel. In 1703, John Burwash, George Fuller and William Snipp, described as 'part of the old gang who were owlers in the late war' were taken with contraband at Lydd. They were accused of being in open communication with French sloops and of being in sympathy with the cause of the Jacobites — which former suspicion was incidentally by no means confined to the owlers; as is pointed out in *Something to Declare* (Smith, 1980), many Customs and Excise officers were under the same cloud. Two more notorious (an oft-used adjective in official reports) smugglers were captured soon after; Thomas Bigg and Jacob Walter had just come ashore from a French sloop lying off Dungeness. They were manacled and taken to the George at Lydd where they were put under an armed guard:

> 'They was in a chamber, 6 officers with them, 20 firelocks loaded with powder and ball. At 5 on Sunday night 9 men well mounted & as well armed with pistols, swords, cooper's adzes, wood bills, forks &c comes up to ye house, dismounts from their horses and runs upstairs, firing all ye way . . . wounded 3 officers and got between the

The North Foreland Lighthouse in 1824, as Charles Dickens would have known it. (Old print)

officers and their arms and carried away Walter & Bigg; if these 9 men had not carried them off, a 100 more was hard by ready to make another attack . . . '

Walter was not to enjoy his liberty for very long; he was soon recaptured and taken off to London (see p.66).

An optimistic report from Baker in 1703 raised false hopes in the Exchequer's breast: 'I do believe the neck of the owling trade, as well as the spirit of the owlers, is in great measure broke, especially in Romney Marsh.' He continues by recommending a reduction of the riding officer establishment and their replacement by cavalry patrols with an estimated annual saving of £1,500. Even at the time he wrote, his optimism was not to pass unchallenged. With some temerity, a junior Customs official at Folkestone, Walter Devereux, wrote to a superior at Customs House London:

'Mr Henry Baker, who has the management of the coasts of Kent and Sussex (though he only comes there once or twice a year) has the face, I hear, to set forth that he has stopped exportation in Kent & Sussex . . . '

Devereux continues by offering to produce statistics supplied by the owlers themselves utterly refuting the claim. The man's foolhardy outspokenness cost him his job, while the fact remains that smuggling did abate — but only while Baker remained in charge. Immediately following his withdrawal it flared up again with renewed vigour (1725) and again, during the War of American Independence (1775-83), when it was, briefly, as flourishing a concern as ever.

The Golden Epoch

Good days them, when a man might smuggle honest, didn't have to go a-thieving and weren't afraid to die for his principles.

This sentiment, said to have been expressed by an ancient Deal boatman, is not surprisingly the direct antithesis of Admiral Vernon's ('Old Grog') attitude to the trade. He wrote to the Admiralty in 1745:

'I can't but think 'tis a seasonable time to suggest to your Lordships that there are said to be in the town of Deal no less than two hundred able young men and seafaring people who are known to have no visible way of getting a living but by the infamous trade of smuggling, many keeping a horse and arms to be ready for all calls. At Dover, it is conjectured that there may be as many as four hundred at a time ready to smuggle, at Ramsgate and Folkestone three hundred each . . . about six or seven days past, a Dover cutter landed goods in the night under the Castle, that was carried off by a party of sixty horses . . . This smuggling has converted those employed in it, first from honest industrious fishermen to lazy, drunken, profligate smugglers, and now to dangerous spies on all our proceedings, for the enemy's daily information . . . I can't but think it a national reproach upon us, to have let their villainy & treachery run to such extensive lengths . . . '

War with the Dutch broke out in 1688 and with it, predictably, taxation rocketed. Until this time, import smuggling compared with owling had been regarded as little more than a nuisance but now, with the stupendous tax increases upon consumer goods, the situation changed overnight. Concurrent with the change in taxation came a revolution in naval design; the introduction of the fore-and-aft (i.e. yacht) rig was soon to displace the old square ship rig in the smaller vessels. This conferred far greater manoeuvrability, permitting a much speedier turn-around when unloading the goods. These two happenings were indeed the keys which unlocked the door of the New Age, the Golden Epoch when 'part soldier, part sailor, part trader, the new model smuggler emerged' (*Contraband Cargoes*, N. Williams, 1959). Many who now embarked upon this new style free-trading saw little morally wrong in cheating the revenue; it

(Old print)

A representation of smugglers breaking open the King's Custom House at Poole.

The Mermaid Inn, Rye. A favourite retreat of smugglers, just over the county border.
(see p.39)
(Reproduced by kind permission of the artist, Mr. S. J. Heady of Hastings.)

38

was indeed not for another hundred years that dealing in smuggled goods (as opposed to landing them) was to be declared illegal. Respectable businessmen, squires, parsons and even magistrates were all, indirectly at least, involved in the Wicked Trade from Rumney Marsh (as Defoe called it) and it is in this period that we start to find the best records of the infamous smuggling associations which were to plague Kent for the next hundred years and more.

Often the smuggling gang was named after the locality upon which it was centred, although frequently it covered a far greater area than its name implied — the Hawkhurst gang for example ranged far and wide across the Weald down into Hampshire and Dorset. In Rye, Sussex, they came and went much as they pleased; after a good 'run' they would often repair to the Mermaid Inn to relax 'carousing and smoaking their pipes, with loaded pistols lying on the table before them, no magistrate daring to interfere . . . '

The term 'gang' should perhaps not be taken too literally, or at any rate confined to its nucleus of full-time skilled professionals who would recruit their labour from villages, often many miles distant, on an *ad hoc* basis for a night's work on a preconceived plan. A lantern glow or similar signal would be given (sometimes a struck flint spark sufficed) to indicate the spot where the goods might be safely landed. Here would be mustered the tub-carriers and the 'batsmen'; a cargo of eighty tubs or half-ankers (each containing about four gallons of spirits) would have called for forty men, carrying two each slung by ropes over chest and back. According to circumstances, the goods would be either carried off inland or, if the distance were great, they might go on horseback, each man with an extra led horse carrying an extra three or four tubs. Sometimes with carts and horses available, the full eight gallon anker would be used. The tub-men were not paid on any other basis than hire for the job of carrying heavy weights throughout the night, nevertheless in sheer self-defence they were quite prepared to fight off any opposition and to this end the more war-like were often armed with 'bats'—stout oak or ash cudgels over six foot long. Thus was formed the 'fighting party' of 'batsmen' whose function was to screen the unloading tubmen against interference by any over-zealous revenue man. The going rate in 1800 for a batsman was a guinea a night with the less dangerous role of ordinary tubman commanding 7/6.

At the 'sharp end' of the Trade, one would have found two distinctly different types of smuggler; one at sea and the other on land and usually the two roles did not combine. The more popular type, at least with the popular writers, was the sea-smuggler for they found him the more likeable and romantic. He it was who braved the perils of the deep, dark, dangerous ocean in a daring bid to bring the ladies of quality their silks, lace and perfume; nor was the ordinary citizen's more prosaic but equally necessary dram of spirits, pipe of 'baccy and his good wife's dish of tea to be overlooked—was it not the good Queen Anne herself who was one of the first to yield to the relaxing charms of that beverage?

> 'Great Anna, whom three realms obey,
> Doth sometimes counsel take, and sometimes tay,
> (Alexander Pope, 1688-1744, *The Rape of the Lock*)

Lord Teignmouth, co-author of *The Smugglers* (possibly still the best general book on the subject), waxed lyrical over the sea-smuggler; paradoxical but perhaps understandable when it is recalled that he was once a commander in Queen Victoria's Navy and later an Inspector of her Coastguard:

> 'We do not find the hardy sea-faring smugglers often behaving with the cold-blooded cruelty displayed as a usual phenomenon by the generally unemotional men of the ploughed fields and rustic communities who took up the running and carried the goods inland from the water's edge whither those sea-dogs had brought them. In the being of men who dared tempestuous winds and waves there existed as a rule a more sportsmanlike and generous spirit. Something of the traditional heartiness

inseparable from sea life impelled them to give and take without that black blood which seethed evilly in the veins of landsmen. The seaman, it seemed, realised that smuggling was a risk; something in the nature of any game of skill into which they entered, with the various officers of the law naturally opposed to them; and when either side won, that was incidental to the game, and no enmity followed as the matter of course it was with their shore-going partners.'

Another of the old school, Captain E. P. Brenton RN (*A History of the Royal Navy*) also pays the sea-smuggler high compliments:

'These men are as remarkable for their skill as for their audacity in the hour of danger; their local knowledge has been highly advantageous to the Navy, into which, however, they never enter unless sent on board ships of war as a punishment for some crime committed against the revenue laws. They are hardy, sober and faithful to each other beyond the generality of seamen; when shipwreck occurs they have been known to perform deeds not exceeded in any country of the world . . . '

Other writers held the same opinion as Admiral Vernon (see p.37) but in general it appears that the sea-smuggler was seen as the individual pitting strength and skill against Nature as well as against the Customs, whereas the landsman was more of a mere cypher, a hired member of a gang, a nameless, faceless yokel, little other than a broad back and a strong pair of arms to carry away the goods brought over at such risk by the seaman. An over-simplification perhaps, but it certainly seems that no crime committed by the Kentish sea-smuggler ever approached the violence and horror of the land-smugglers of, for instance, the Hawkhurst gang.

It was quite possible for a man in a small way of business to be both land and sea-smuggler; such an individual was Edward Roots of Rochester who in 1727-28 made nine successful cross-Channel trips, returning each time with 500lbs

(Old print)

Rochester. This shows the sort of craft Roots would have owned. (see p.41)

of tea which meant for him a gross return of £1,600 (besides defrauding the Revenue of £670)—and this at a time when a London labourer if lucky could make 10/- a week. Roots' sloop *Mermaid* carried a crew of six, which included himself and his brother Richard; they had several narrow escapes. On one return run, they were chased by the Herne Bay revenue cutter for over three hours, escaping by a whisker when the cutter's cross-yard snapped. Later that year, after another trip, *Mermaid* was taken, but Roots got clean away with the goods and soon fitted out a new sloop the *John & Mary* and was back in business not long after.

His tea landed, Roots' next task was to get it away off the beach as soon as he was able; this was done by putting it in a cart and making for Blackheath, a not too arduous 'carry' of some twenty miles. Here it was hidden, either in the grounds of the Duke of Montagu's country mansion (with the active connivance of 'Yorkshire Tom' the head gardener) or else in the bushes and brambles at Shooter's Hill crossroads, then still the haunt of footpads and highwaymen as Hasted (1797) the greatest Kent historian tells us:

> 'It was always a place of much dread and danger to travellers, owing to the narrowness of the road over it and the continual lurking nests of thieves among the woods and coppices . . . it was impossible for a traveller, waylaid, to escape falling into the ruffians' hands, which gave occasion to continual robberies being committed here, even at noonday.'

At one or the other of these secluded spots then, well away from prying eyes, Roots would rendezvous with his middle-men—or, in his case—ladies, of whom there were four trusted regulars. Three were housewives all living in Smithfield; the fourth Mrs Cowie, landlady of the Boot inn, Deptford, a place of some importance as a Royal dockyard since the time of Henry VIII and by Roots' day 'a large and populous town with 3,500 houses and 15,000 inhabitants, a great part of it inhabited by people of good fashion and credit' (Hasted). Their

(Old print)

A place of much dread and danger . . .
Execution at Shooter's Hill, 19th August 1805. George Webb and Richard Russell hanged for house-breaking at Deptford, Eltham and New Cross. Webb, son of a clergyman, was a deserter from the West Kent Militia and also a smuggler. Russell an ex-sailor turned butcher, turned brickmaker, was 'a most industrious man'.

The grid-like structure in the background was part of the Admiralty shutter signalling system which, given good visibility, could transmit a message from Deal to Whitehall in, so it is said, under four minutes. To its right is seen Severndroog Castle which despite its antique appearance was then barely twenty years old; it was erected by the widow of Sir William James to commemorate his capture of Severndroog fortress on the Malabar coast of India. Almost as high as the dome of St. Paul's, the tower was used as a triangulation point in the Great Survey of England 1848.

business transactions completed, the ladies would depart, their precious burdens 'secure in packets tied beneath their petticoats' where, presumably, before the days of sexual harassment, no revenue officer however brave would have essayed to peer. Besides the notorious Groombridge, Hawkhurst and Mayfield associations, there were plenty of smaller concerns flourishing within their own little patches. One such was the Callis Court gang, run by Joss Snelling from his cottage at Broadstairs. Joss Bay, a favourite bathing beach, perpetuates his name; a tunnel running from Callis Court down to the beach was precipitously rediscovered in 1954 when a bulldozer fell through its roof. One of the most notorious 'affrays' (this was the official term for describing engagements between the revenue men and smugglers) took place early in Joss Snelling's career. One dark night early in 1769, the gang turned out at full strength to unload the lugger *Lark* at Kingsgate. Attacked while so engaged by a force of revenue men, Snelling and four others escaped by scaling the cliff behind them. Having gained the top, they were challenged by a lone riding officer, who paid dearly for his courage. Having shot him dead, the five made their way to safety across what is now the golf course. Following the encounter, still known as the Battle of Botany Bay, a house search was made in the hamlet of Reading Street; two smugglers, one dead and the other dying, were found in Rosemary Cottage. Nine were killed in the pursuit and six taken alive, later to hang in Gallows Field, Sandwich.

Undeterred by this setback, Snelling persisted and returned to trading the next year, his gang increased to double its previous strength. Snelling never 'reformed'; at the age of 90 he was convicted of smuggling and fined £100. At about the same time, he was presented to the young Princess (later Queen) Victoria as 'The famous Broadstairs Smuggler' when she visited the area in 1829. He was to die peacefully in his bed at the age of 96, no doubt comforted by the thought that the family business was not to fold up — both his son George and

Joss Snelling's cottage today.

grandson Jim were in the Trade, too.

Sir John Sawbridge, smuggler, squire and magistrate, lived in Warden Manor in the Isle of Sheppey during the closing years of the 18th century. The smoking room (now the library) of his house was heavily shuttered and it contained a pigeon loft, cunningly concealed. Smugglers entering the Swale estuary used to throw overboard the suitably protected contraband which would float and drift on the tide into Barrows Brook inlet. Simultaneously a carrier pigeon would be released which on arrival at the smoking room would alert the occupants so that a suitable pick-up could be arranged. Once, so the legend goes, Sir John was out collecting cargo when he was surprised by revenue men. Managing to evade his pursuers, he made hell for leather to the Manor and, rushing to his bedchamber dived beneath the counterpane still belted, booted and spurred; naturally, when the King's men hammered at his door he was fast asleep. On the anniversary of his escape, Sir John's ghost may be seen galloping madly through the woods along the route to freedom.

A better authenticated example may be cited to illustrate

the wide spectrum of classes involved in smuggling. An anonymous letter to the Customs Commissioners gives details of the smugglers' casualties in an affray at Bulverhythe (Sussex) in March 1737 and continues:

> 'I can send a List of the names of the Persons that were at that Business . . . young Mr Bowra was not there, but his men and horses were and a Custom House Officer took some Tea and Arms too at Bowra's house at Groombridge . . . young Bowra's House cost £500 abuilding *(a vast sum for those days)* and he will pay for looking up . . . Morten and Bowra sold, last Winter, someways about 3,000lbs *(of tea)* a week.'

Flemish gable-end of a row of cottages in Reading Street. (see p.45)

Local evidence makes it plain that the 'young Bowra' was John, born at Groombridge in 1713; his grandfather Thomas Bowra was a surgeon of Sevenoaks, a nearby market town and his father, John, was a Groombridge churchwarden. Young John was a land surveyor, destined to map many a west Kent estate for local gentry. One of his earliest works, executed not long after the exploits hinted at above, was a survey of Tunbridge Wells, dedicated to Lord Abergavenny, one of the leading local landowners. This little masterpiece, beautifully drawn and exquisitely coloured, still exists in the British Library.

Rosemary Cottage today.
(see p.45)

48

Against such a respectable background one might, were one not familiar with the ways of the Trade, have been surprised to find that later in 1737 young Bowra found himself in court, charged with carrying off tea which had been landed between Pevensey and Eastbourne and transporting it into Ashdown Forest. His home village of Groombridge figures in the evidence thus:

> 'A place several years noted for entertaining and harbouring the most notorious desperate persons concerned in carrying on the Smuggling Trade in defiance of the Laws, and got to such a height of insolence that there was a necessity of sending down a detachment of soldiers to curb them, for they strick terrour into the inhabitants of that part of the country.'

Cecil Bowra, John's collateral descendant, comments *(Archaeologia Cantiana* Vol 83):

> 'So far as the young man was concerned, at any rate we may conclude that a lesson was learned from this youthful indiscretion and his activities thenceforth confined to the peaceful pursuit of his profession.'

Cove Cottage, St. Peter's Broadstairs derives its name from three smugglers' caves in the garden where this picture was taken.

49

Gallows Field, Sandwich.   Horses graze where malefactors once suffered.

Warden Manor, Sheppey.   Once the home of Sir John Sawbridge. (see p.46)

One may indeed hope so, but one may have some reservations. At much the same time and only a few miles away, Daniel Barker, the Customs officer at Tonbridge, was being given a very hard time:

'We are very much infested with Smuglers that goe in such large Bodies armed with Blunderbusses and other offencive weapons, several of which have called at my House, swaring they would kill me or any other Officer they should meet with. About a fortnight past we had an Excise Officer of Seven Okes was taken prisoner . . . last night Mr Griffin, Supervisor of Excise, was beatt and Cutt in so Violent a manor that his life is Dispar'd of by a Large Parcell of Smuglers within a mile of Tunbridge. They likewise beat & Misuses severall Private People in the road, making them kneel down in the mud & beg their Pardons. Sir, I humbly Beg your utmost Endevours we may be suply'd with some Soldiers.'

Sometimes the rival gangs would co-operate, especially if

Warden Point, Sheppey.
Erosion here takes place at a galloping 9′ every year (1964). Elsewhere on the northern coast of Sheppey the rate is 3′ (1962).

51

there was a really large cargo to handle. There exists plenty of evidence showing that the Kent traders were in collusion with other counties, especially in East Anglia—perhaps the ancient links of Yarmouth with the Cinque Ports in the herring trade had something to do with this. A good instance is given in a Custom House letter to the Collector at Blakeney and Clay:

'I think it is the duty of every Friend to his Country to think seriously of the Trade now carried on with our Enemies and at Dunkirk by several large cutters belonging to Folkestone and Hastings, and are authorised by Letters of Marque *(a licence given, or rather sold, to a merchant vessel permitting it to attack enemy shipping)* from England & French passes from France. Thomas Wood is now going to Dunkirk in a large cutter of 200 tons, deep waisted, mounts 16 carriage guns, carries 40 men and to take in a cargo of tea value 7 to 8,000 Pounds: his track to land these goods is between Dunwich & Orfordness; the firm of the House is Pinfold & Provo (Provo is a Frenchman and lives at Dunkirk, Pinfold lives at Folkestone and John Minter of Folkestone is one concerned in the House). Robert Tapley trades to Dunkirk in a cutter 180 tons, 14 guns & 40 men, he trades to Cornwall & sometimes to the Yorkshire coast. One Anthony Warmer of Folkestone trades to Dunkirk in a cutter 90 tons; Mark Bayley of Hastings & Solomon Bevel trade to Dunkirk in a large cutter near 200 tons of 14 guns and land their goods between Beachy Head and Shoreham; cargoes worth 4, 5 to 6,000 Pounds.

To the Collector & Comptroller of Clay. Pay particular attention & communicate the same to the Riding Officers & Preventive Officers & to the Commanders of the Cruizers with strict injunctions to use their best endeavours & to Prevent the clandestine trade & punish the offenders.

Edward Stanley, Customs House, London 22 May 1781.'

Co-operation between rival gangs would sometimes lead to internecine strife, such as was witnessed by the Canterbury Superintendent of Customs:

'1st April 1746. Such a scene happened yesterday in Wingham Street that I believe nothing like of the sort has, since Creation . . . '

It appears that three separate bands, one from Sussex, one from Folkestone and the third the ill-famed Hawkhurst gang, had got together to unload a monster consignment of eleven and a half tons of tea somewhere near Herne Bay. Having loaded this amount onto 350 pack-horses, a further eight tons remained for them to deal with a little further along the coast. It had been previously agreed that all should stay in the vicinity until all were loaded up, but 'everyone got his load and shifted for himself as soon as it were possible.' The Sussex and the Hawkhurst men considered themselves betrayed by the others and, much put out, returned to their home bases, only to hasten back considerably reinforced with 'nearly an Hundred men all armed with Fuzees, pistols & Broad-swords . . . they fight with Swords, two men wounded and two very much so. At last Sussex & Hawkhurst were masters of ye field and carried off 40 horses belonging to Folkestone.' Any unfortunate passer-by was relieved of his purse, 'ye dogges were so attrociously inclin'd . . . they at last went to Waldershire, but where now, I have not heard . . . '

Another report from the same source makes it very clear that it was far from easy to persuade anyone to testify against the Traders:

'When ye fellow *(a potential witness for the Crown)* parted from me, he was almost dead with fear, having been shot at and his horse wounded, he now lives a most shocking life . . . '

Even when a man was found willing to stand up in Court, the difficulties of the Solicitor-General were by no means ended:

'Ye person who is Solicitor for ye Smugglers when in

Newgate is one Kelly, an Irish Roman Catholick. He has ye assurance from his country and his principles from his religion, or from Hell itself; and to make a gentleman so accomplished compleatly a man of business, he has 40 or 50 of his own country and religion at his command who are ever ready to sware whatever he cares to dictate.'

It has been sometimes remarked that the local clergy of the time were, to say the least, hesitant to interfere with their parishioners' business interests but in all fairness it is difficult to see what they could have done even had they wished to protest. Sometimes, however, a man of the cloth was stirred into action. Early in 1746, a party some hundred and fifty strong ran a cargo between Reculver and Birchington and made their way inland, some with eighty horses passing by way of Whitstable and Faversham with the rest crossing the Stour at Grove Ferry. Their movements were reported to the

Pegwell Bay, Ramsgate.
Yesterday, a favourite landing spot for smugglers; today, the cooling towers of Richborough power station stand sentinel in place of the Coast Blockade.

Customs Commissioners by the Revd Mr Patten, Vicar of Whitstable, his report being annotated:

> 'That he did formerly receive tythe from ye smugglers but these gangs being such 'rugged colts' (as the Dr calls them) that nothing is to be got from them, which made him angry.'

At the century's turn, a Sussex vicar, the Revd Robert Hardy, Chaplain to the Prince Regent, puts the smuggling situation in a nutshell with his pamphlet, somewhat sonorously entitled *Serious Cautions & Advice to All concerned in Smuggling, setting forth the Mischiefs attendant upon that Traffic, together with some Exhortations to Patience & Contentment under the Difficulties & Trials of Life.* Although his observations emanated from over the county border, there is no reason to doubt that Mr Hardy's conclusions were equally as valid for Kent as for Sussex. He placed the smugglers into three categories, viz:

(i) Those employing their capital in the Trade
(ii) Those doing the work
(iii) Those dealing in contraband, either as dealers or consumers.

Wingham Street today.

A scene of idyllic peace shattered 1st April 1746. (see p.53)   (Old print)

He was convinced that smuggling was not confined to the lower classes but 'from what I have heard, I apprehend that it has very generally been encouraged by their superiors for whom no manner of excuse that I know of can be offered . . . '

John Wesley (1703-81) also denounced the Trade in no uncertain terms. In a sermon at Rye he spoke with his usual fiery courage: 'Every smuggler is a thief-general who picks the pockets both of the King and all his fellow subjects. He wrongs them all.' Wesley was right in supposing that his strictures would fall on deaf ears.

The Bloody End

> We all went down to the sea-shore,
> Our company behind and the batsmen before:
> I thought that the game would not long last,
> Our batsmen went on much too fast:
> For to kill a man is a very bad thing,
> When out on duty and serving the King.

(Trad.)

With the final defeat of Napoleon at Waterloo, the Trade was immediately affected in two ways. Firstly, the Royal Navy, now no longer concerned with watching the French, was enabled to turn again to the smuggler with renewed zest and application. Secondly, however, to counter this fact, a quarter of a million discharged servicemen, trained to some degree in the art of war but little else besides, were pouring back into civilian life. There being little in the way of retraining schemes, most had to rely on chance to find a living, although it is only fair to mention such official work schemes which did employ ex-servicemen, albeit only temporarily; one such was the lowering (by pick and shovel) of the crest of Shooter's Hill to ease the passage of traffic along the road to Dover. Many chose to emigrate and played their part in opening up our new British Empire; others chose to stay at home to go 'on the parish', tramping the country and existing on charity. Thousands more, 'the most daring professional men discharged from their occupation and adverse to the daily labour of agricultural or mechanical employment (were to become) the ready instruments of those desperate persons who have a little capital and are hardy enough to engage in the trade of smuggling.' This Treasury Report was to prove only too accurate and smuggling rose to unprecedented heights, more in Kent than anywhere else in the entire country.

With commendable but uncharacteristic speed, the government reacted and within one year of Waterloo the Coast Blockade for the Prevention of Smuggling was ready for action. Comprised entirely of naval personnel, it took over the entire responsibility for patrolling the Kent and Sussex coasts to settle the free-traders' account once and for all or, as its commander was to put it, 'to make the grass grow in the streets of Deal.' Soon, the Kent gangs came to realise that the Royal Navy was not bluffing and that unless the Blockade were challenged and forced to withdraw, the days of Trading were over. More and more, fire-arms became the order of the day — pistols, muskets, blunderbusses, duck-guns — whatever

The twin towers remain today, just as useful to the modern navigator as they were in Trading days.

(Old print)

came to hand was put to deadly use. The coast from Sheerness to Pevensey and beyond echoed and re-echoed to the clash of cutlass, the rattle of musketry and the whine of the ricochet, the shouts of anger and alarm, the howls of the wounded, the groans of the dying. The old order of the Gentlemen was to perish in a final cloud of gunsmoke and in a welter of blood.

Typical of this savage period was George Ransley (ca1780-1856), last and best known leader of the Aldington gang (otherwise known as the South Kents or the Blues) which flourished on Romney Marsh in the early 1800s. Equipped with brains, brawn and capital, he was possessed of undeniable style and panache but perhaps does not really rate as a master-smuggler if only because he was too much concerned with the Trade's mechanics and grass-roots. His personal charisma ensured that most who knew him liked him well; with a family name already a by-word in the annals of Marsh smuggling (see *Smuggling — The Wicked Trade*) he must have had a head start in his chosen vocation. Starting life as a farm boy, with a peculiar affinity with horses, it was not long before he became carter at Court Lodge Farm, Aldington and it was here that he was caught in the act of stealing corn — for his horses. No charge was brought against him; his employer must have sensibly realised that unfortunate 'accidents' were liable to occur to the stock, crops and buildings of those with the temerity to tangle with such as George.

After his marriage (into another Marsh smuggling family) Ransley quit the land to take up full-time smuggling, succeeding to the gang leadership after the famous Brookland affray of 1822. The Blues' main headquarters was the Walnut Tree inn at Aldington where the room in which it is said they laid many of their schemes may be seen to this day. Ransley's house, the Bourne Tap, is also still standing, inhabited and restored, on Aldington Frith. In his day, it was a popular rendezvous, people would flock there from miles around, on foot, on horseback or in carts, to collect their liquor allocations. Very often, they would partake on the spot and a

An Edwardian postcard of Sandwich.

merry party would ensue; as an eye-witness put it: 'They would dance around, drunk and half-naked, I can name them!'

Time ran out for the South Kents in 1826; having shot and killed a Blockade petty officer on Dover beach, they were hunted down by Lt Samuel Hellard RN who with a force of one hundred men and accompanied by two Bow Street runners raided Aldington one stormy autumn night to catch them all in their beds. All were tried and sentenced to death but some smart work by their attorney enabled them to cheat the holiday crowd waiting to watch them swing on Penenden Heath; their sentence was commuted to transportation for life to Van Diemen's Land (now Tasmania) where many were joined by their wives and families to make what fresh starts they could. After several years all who survived were pardoned on condition that they never returned home; Ransley, reunited eventually with his wife and ten children, reverted to farming, settling down on 500 rented acres at River Plenty, Hobart and living out the rest of his days there; he died 'respected and loved by all who knew him'.

It was the privilege of Lydd on Romney Marsh to witness the last of the big Kentish 'runs' of contraband. Early one winter's morning in 1829 twelve laden carts escorted by eighty free-traders, all armed to the teeth, rumbled through the main street to the ringing cheers of the populace; with this spectacle the traditional 'open' method of running the goods had run its course and the more clandestine methods came to predominate. This did not, however, signify the end of 'trading'; on the contrary, it persisted so much that many thought to blame smugglers for the agricultural wage riots and the machine breaking of the early 1830s in which Kentish labourers played a predominant part. Some went as far as accusing them of importing revolutionary ideas from France (where Louis Philippe 'the People's King' had just been set up); Zachary Pilcher of Sandwich was one of these, he expressed his fears in the *Kentish Gazette*: 'A force of 100,000 men, all trained in the use of weapons, could be raised to march on London . . . ' These fears were happily not realised—it is very doubtful that the Trade was involved at all—and life went on much as before until industry, in the shape of brickfields, cement works and the railway, itself invaded the Garden of England.

The Old Bull Inn, Shooters Hill.
From a water-colour by George Scharf (1826) and reproduced from *An Account of the Road Works on Shooters Hill 1816* by F. C. Elliston-Erwood FSA (Vol XXVIII Reports of the Woolwich and District Antiquarian Society 1947). The lowering of the crest (see p.57) is well illustrated.

The beginning and end of a letter to John Collier (see p.65) from the Customs Commissioners in London, requiring him to investigate a charge by the Supervisor at Ashford that Thomas Jordan, a revenue officer at Folkestone, was purchasing contraband from the Dragoons stationed there.

From the Collier Papers and reproduced by kind permission of R. Sayer, Esq.

NB The signatory Sir John Evelyn was the grandson of the diarist. He held office from 1721 to 1769 and had great political power, being connected by marriage with the Godolphin family.

Smuggler Chasers

*Will Washington take America or the Smugglers
England first? The bet would be a fair, even one.*

(Lord Pembroke, 1781)

The establishment of governmental anti-smuggling forces
was initiated by the reorganisation of the Customs in 1671, but
these forces were not always very effective. Poor leaders and
bad communications apart, quite often the bulk of our regular
forces were heavily committed elsewhere in Europe or in North
America, hence the remark quoted above. Perforce, then,
anti-smuggling operations were of low priority, but that is not
to say that they were never undertaken.

Soldiers versus Smugglers

*I am sorry to say that there are some officers who
never desire to make a campaign except against the
smugglers, some who would be much better pleased
to watch all night for the seizure of tea and brandy
than to march into the trenches, and I do assure you
that they had much rather be commanded by a
Custom House Officer than Prince Eugene or the
Duke of Marlborough.*

(Letter to the *Monthly Intelligence* 1737
signed 'Old Soldier')

Despite this old warrior's strictures, the overall military
presence was often quite effective; it was noted that when the
Revenue were backed by the presence of cavalry, as at

Canterbury, Lydd and Folkestone, the seizures were far greater than in the less well patrolled parts of the county; this observation is rather discounted by another early report on Dragoons posted on Romney Marsh:

'What Assistance they gave was chiefly to the Owlers; they left their Stable Doors open, upon compact with ye Exporters, to give them an Opportunity of making use of their Horses in ye Night-Time, for conveying the Wool to the Sea-side where ye Shallops lay ready to receive it.'

At about that time, owling was made a felony, punishable by death. This rather incensed the Marsh traders who took up fire-arms in place of bludgeons 'so that none dare meddle with them without five files of soldiers'. Over the following years, the Marsh was to see plenty of cavalry; troops were quartered at Folkestone, Dymchurch, New Romney, Lydd and East Guldeford. Further inland, there were detachments of the Queen's Dragoons at Canterbury and Ashford, subsequently replaced by the Earl of Essex's Regiment. It was at this time early in the 18th century that Daniel Defoe passing through Kent made his famous observation:

'As I rode along this coast I perceived several dragoons, riding officers and others, armed and on horseback, riding always as if they were huntsmen beating up their game; upon enquiry I found their diligence was in quest of owlers, as they call them, and sometimes they catch some of them but when I come to enquire further I find too that oftentimes they are attacked in the night with such numbers that they dare not resist them or, if they do, as it were, do stand still and see the wool carried off before their faces, not daring to interfere.'

The private soldier on anti-smuggling duty was supposed to receive twopence extra daily, but payment was often tardy and irregular; in 1708 the Queen's Dragoons were still owed £625.10.0 although they had quit the Marsh two years previously; they had, however, been made a special allowance of £200 'to replace Stockings worn out in pursuit of

John Collier.

Surveyor-General of the Riding Officers for the County of Kent (1733-56). A Hastings attorney, he was also land agent for the East Sussex estate of the Duke of Newcastle.

This portrait is owned by a direct descendant, R. Sayer Esq of Walsingham, and is reproduced by his kind permission.

Much of Collier's correspondence with the Customs Commissioners in London is preserved in the Sayer ms in the East Sussex Archives. It is obvious that he had to tread a careful path between the letter of the Law that he was paid to represent and the reactions of his neighbours and relatives by marriage, some of whom were in the Trade.

He appears as a likeable character, not without humour and compassion; this underlines the general principle that people were often more humane than the laws they lived under. For instance, five convicted smugglers, one English and four French, were unable to pay their fines and consequently had been confined in Horsham gaol for more than a year — 'They really all five lye in a very miserable starving condition, not having shirts to their backs, nor hardly any other cloathes . . . they have been in Gaol a year . . . if 'tis possible for any such offenders to be reclaim'd by suffering in Gaole, as the matter appears to me, these persons will never committ any more Crimes of this nature . . . I gave them 10/- amongst them to help towards their subsistence. They told me it was more than they have had since they have been here before.'

Smugglers'. When owling on the Marsh declined in 1706, troops were withdrawn, only to be recalled in 1720 when the Trade took an upward turn. A financial inducement to keenness was then offered, in the shape of a reward given for the capture of contraband, but this was not as attractive a carrot as it might have been; the money was shared throughout the entire regiment according to rank so that the lower ranks upon whom fell the brunt of the work stood to profit the least and this predictably dulled their enthusiasm. Officers fared somewhat better, the commander of the troops taking Walter following the fracas at the George, Lydd (see p.34) was commended for his action (large amounts of brandy and a number of horses were also taken) and he was awarded £200.

Even when in the fairly close vicinity, the soldiers were not always in a position to help the revenue men, as the Folkestone riding officer discovered to his cost on New Year's Day 1744 when, in dire need of assistance, he sent word to the commander of the nearest troops at Dover; his plea was declined on the grounds that it would entail a march of more than five miles — understandable perhaps when one pictures the state of the roads at that time of year. By 1730, the import smuggling of brandy and tea had surpassed owling in economic importance; the smugglers 'growing to such a height of insolence as to carry their wicked practices by force and violence not only in the country and remote parts of the Kingdom, but even in the City of London itself' (Findings of a Parliamentary Committee, 1733).

The owlers took more and more to firearms — 'fuzees charged with gunpowder and leaden bullets' — and soon the hapless Customs officers and magistrates found the situation completely out of control 'even by the assistance of such regular forces as have been sent to our aid'. Dragoons were called out at Groombridge (see p.49) and the Hawkhurst gang ravaged the Weald and far beyond. At Ashford, a barn was searched with half a ton of tea and a considerable quantity of silks and velvet being recovered; while the goods were being loaded on to wagons for transport to London, under an armed guard, fifty smugglers attacked. Losing two of their number, 'they thought fit to retire, having first fired the barn.' Similar incidents were to follow; an escort of riding officers, troopers and a sergeant from the Tower were escorting a coachload of recovered contraband tea through Lewisham to the Customs House in London. They were ambushed by four smugglers 'brandishing blunderbusses, cutlasses and pistols, swearing and shouting'; the smugglers killed one horse, but return fire was more lethal with two of them killed and one captured. On another occasion at Limpsfield, Revenue officers and dragoons set a trap which resulted in the recovery of half a ton of tea and the capture of seven horses. The whole military responsibility in Kent at the time fell upon thirty-nine dragoons and nine companies of infantry; John Collier (see p.65) pleaded and importuned as best he could for at least two hundred more troopers. After many appeals, three Marine detachments were detailed to augment the hard-pressed Marsh riding officers, but Mr Claire, Supervisor of Riding Officers at Hythe, had grave reservations:

'I know not how to proceed . . . considering they are foot soldiers and therefore not of that service to the officers in the Customs as dragoons would be. Then, should I apply to the commanding officer at Canterbury for a detachment of his men to act against the smugglers? If I have not an hundred men to plant at Lydd, Romney, Dymchurch and Hythe, it will signify nothing, for, unless I have a number at first sufficient to make head against such numbers as there are (and so well armed), I should only be the cause of men's coming to the coast to be knocked on the head, which will make them more insolent than they are now.'

Fanny Burney, the 18th century diarist, called Deal a 'sad, smuggling town'; certainly its reputation for free-trading was second to none and the place was seldom far from the minds of

Deal Castle Kent.

(Old print)

those in authority, as a *Morning Post* report of 31st October 1781 bears witness:

'Just before daybreak four Irish independent companies and two of the Middlesex Militia arrived from Dover, conducted by two Customs-house officers armed with extraordinary powers who began to break into the houses. A large quantity of uncustomed goods were soon found and many waggonloads conducted to Deal Castle. You will hardly imagine that this was done with much tranquillity and, lest nine companies should not be sufficient, above one hundred of Lord Sheffield's Horse came into town during the affair. I can not describe the scene, but it gave me the tolerable idea of the sacking of a town. Some flint and many stones came at the windows and many shots were fired by the soldiers but most miraculously nobody was killed and only one man considerably wounded who, having thrown a mattock-iron from a garden at the officers, a Middlesex militiaman fired at him as he was scrambling over a wall. We passed a most remarkable day and night, every moment upon the brink of mischief, the streets so

Deal From Pier (East).   *An Edwardian postcard.*

crowded with soldiers that they were scarce passable. Many were very glad to see the Light Horse, I believe some supposed that they prevented a massacre . . . '

At first, the townspeople refused to billet the troops, but

'Nothing brought them to reason so effectively as some of the Light Horse leading their mounts into the kitchens and other apartments and beginning to rub them down there . . . '

The soldiers received a total reward of £1,000 for the recovery of contraband, but

'Had they arrived a few hours earlier they would have had the opportunity of seizing immense quantities to the value of £100,000. If the Revenue officers were occasionally assisted by a strong military force, there is no doubt that a great check would be given to practices so injurious to the commercial interests of the Kingdom and so openly carried out that it is a shame and a disgrace to the executive power to suffer them with impunity.'

Three years later (January 1784) the Prime Minister, Pitt the Younger himself, ordered action against the Deal smugglers. It had been a stormy month, atrocious even for that part of the coast and in consequence all craft had been pulled up on to the foreshore, which was completely deserted. On the morning of the 14th, a troop of the 13th Light Dragoons, under personal orders from the Prime Minister, trotted along the Sandwich road into Deal with the intention of destroying the beached luggers. Their plans were already known to the Deal men, for the landlord of the Fig Tree inn at Kingsgate where the troops were quartered had 'happened to overhear' the orders being read out and had sent immediate word by carrier pigeon to his brother who kept the Drum at Walmer (a village just outside Deal). So it was that a force of three hundred smugglers turned out to 'welcome' the Dragoons as they rode in; had it not been for the timely arrival of the 38th Foot which had force-marched from Canterbury to support them, much blood might have been spilt. As it was, every single Deal inn-keeper took down his sign — by so doing he was no longer obliged by law to billet troops — and every private house door was locked, bolted and barred. The Colonel of the 38th was forced to negotiate with a local farmer for the hire of a barn to shelter his weary men (it was mid-January) and this was secured only after long hard bargaining and only then at an exorbitant rental on a two-year lease.

Rested and refreshed the next day the regiment marched down to the beach, ostensibly to practise an anti-invasion drill, this pretence being enhanced by the presence of several RN cutters off the shore. Suddenly, on a shouted command, the soldiers turned to seize each and every vessel drawn up close by on the shingle, smashed them and set them ablaze: 'In the presence of such overwhelming force, the boatmen could make no attempt at rescue and the whole of the luggers was destroyed. Great indeed must have been the mortification of the men at this wicked and wanton destruction of their only means of livelihood' — but whether the writer refers to smuggling or to fishing is not made clear.

Although the foregoing was 'a rap on the knuckles that Deal never forgot', it never really deterred the Traders; in 1801 for example, two revenue cutters *Tartar* and *Lively* intercepted a smuggling vessel close to Deal beach. A brisk fight ensued and the smuggler was boarded and her men driven ashore. As *Lively's* crew started to off-load the goods, a crowd of longshoremen came onto the scene and attacked them. The revenue men retreated under heavy fire with one officer killed and several men badly wounded; by the time the Lancashire Militia arrived it was too late to retrieve the situation — the goods had vanished and so had the mob.

When, as was so often the case, regular forces were otherwise engaged, the Militia units were often called upon to bear the brunt of anti-smuggling operations. The Militia was a body of men conscripted by ballot (service could be avoided by paying another to act as deputy) ostensibly for home defence.

A Riding Officer . . .
'A sad old scoundrel as ever you knew . . . He rode in his stirrups at sixteen stone two'
(R. H. Barham, *Ingoldsby Legends*). One of R. Simpkins' illustrations. (see pp.127
and 131)

Occasionally called out in aid of the civil power to suppress riots, they appear to have been treated with a certain amount of good-humoured ridicule, not unlike a Napoleonic Dads' Army. They were often suspected (as also were the regulars) of helping rather than hindering the smugglers. At times it seems that they actually went out of their way to do so, as at Dungeness where riding officers engaged in retrieving tubs floating off the beach were manhandled by a party of the Flintshire Militia serving there. The War Office tried to counter possible links through family ties by posting units as far away from home counties as possible and this explains why a north countryman met his fate in far-off Deal:

'On 25th September 1794, the Customs officers discovered on a lugger just beached a large amount of contraband but being too weak to seize the boat themselves they called upon the Westmoreland Militia (then quartered in the town) for assistance; the seizure was then made without much opposition and a guard of soldiers left on the beach with the prize. At about one in the morning someone crept near in the darkness and fired point blank at the guard, Private John Elbeck, who fell mortally wounded. The miscreant made off and although the trading community of Deal offered a reward for his arrest he was never discovered.'

. . . and his Best Friend
A government issue percussion pistol (ca 1800). Each riding officer was armed with two of these and a cavalry sabre.

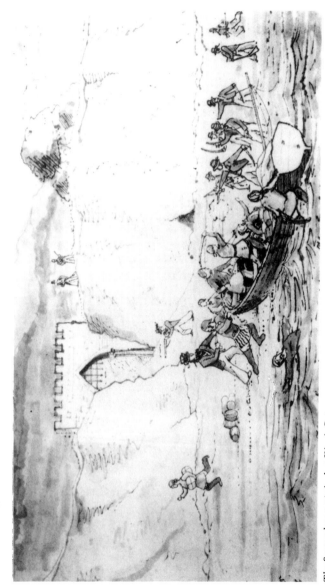

The Smugglers surprised at King's Gate.
An original watercolour by Alan Harper, 1814.
Harper was a Riding Officer patrolling between Herne Bay and Ramsgate, ca 1800. King's Gate — now Kingsgate — was originally a stone gateway erected in 1683 to commemorate the landing of the restored King Charles II and his brother the Duke of York. (see also pp. 21 and 82)

The Landguard

*Of very little Service, 'tho a great Burthen to the
Revenue . . .*

Thus Sir William Musgrave, Commissioner of Customs, in
his Annual Report, 1783, but despite this damning opinion,
the Landguard of Riding Officers was, in the early days, the
backbone of the land forces challenging the smuggler. The
first tentative experiments were made in 1690; two officers
were stationed in each of the four 'hot spots' in or near
Romney Marsh — Lydd, Romney, Hythe and Folkestone — with
a salary of £60 per annum. At the same time the sloops
Enquiry and *Observator* which had been patrolling the coast
were withdrawn in the interests of economy. Eight years later,
further legislation having been introduced in yet another
effort to curb the owlers, the system was extended over the
whole country and the Landguard proper was formed with
299 officers under 17 Senior Surveyors — a force barely
sufficient for the south alone. Stationed at varying intervals
along the coast, according to the nature of the terrain but
averaging about ten miles, the riding officers were armed with
a brace of government-issue pistols and a cavalry sabre and
required to patrol their districts day and night up to a distance
of five miles inland. His pay was increased to £90 yearly, out of
which he provided the keep for his horse and the pay of his
personal servant. Duties specified were: 'To prevent the
carrying of wool to France and the bringing over of
uncustomed and prohibited goods by the French privateers.'
He was expected to maintain a close liaison with fellow officers
on his flanks so that concerted plans could be laid; a Journal
had to be kept in which all his movements and seizures were
logged. These were subject to periodical scrutiny by his
Supervisor who was ordered to investigate all irregularities
which manifested themselves, to report upon them and to
make, if deemed necessary, written charges to go before
higher authority at Customs House, London. Another of the

75

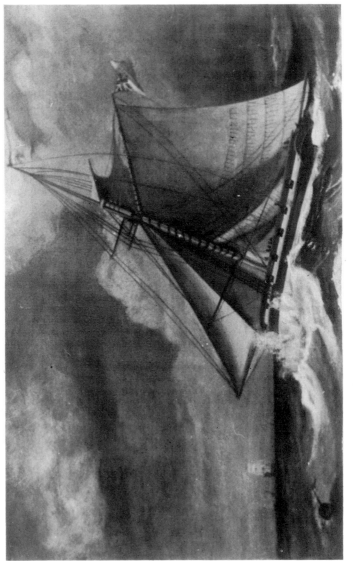

A typical Revenue Cutter of 1800, used during the Suppression of Smuggling, between the period 1780 to 1820.

Supervisor's tasks was to keep in close contact with the commanders of the revenue cruisers operating in his area.

The life of a conscientious riding officer was hard, lonely and often short; bachelors 'without the clog of a family' were preferred, they could be better relied upon for round-the-

Joss Snelling at work unloading a "run" at Kingsgate, circa 1810. The cave is situated below the "Captain Digby" inn.

clock service whereas wives were constantly complaining about the intolerably unsocial hours their husbands were expected to keep. Nevertheless, many officers were married and their wives and families often subjected to brutal intimidation. With violent death an ever-present possibility, it is hardly surprising that many found it expedient to lie low and work out an understanding with those they were expected to harry. No doubt it was such as they whom Commissioner Musgrave had in mind as he continued his Report in the same critical vein:

> 'Of late Years, parliamentary Interest hath recommended Apothecaries, Brewers and other Tradesmen who never ride except when their own occupations require it & fabricate their Journals for the rest of the time. And it is generally reported that many of them are the relation of — & even that some of them are Agents & Collectors for — the Smugglers . . . '

Sometimes, it can not be denied, the riding officer was not above practising the Clandestine Trade himself; two were taken at Folkestone in 1806 unloading goods from the *Nimble* of Deal, herself a revenue cutter. Both were dismissed the Service, retiring most likely to well-feathered nests.

Life was indeed hard for the honest man, but by 1808 his load was lightened to some degree; a widow's and dependants' pension fund was started so that, by the day's standards, the riding officer would at least know that his future, or that of his family, would be secure if he ran into trouble. For the loss of a limb on duty a yearly pension of £15 could be expected, the same to his widow if he were killed, plus £5 yearly for each child under the age of 15. Many officers held on to their posts until they were well into their eighties; even then they were forcibly retired; the rank itself persisted until 1860.

Despite its many shortcomings, the Landguard provided part of the embryo of a properly organised anti-smuggling force which, after many a vicissitude, was eventually to develop into Her Majesty's Coast Guard.

The Waterguard

*The Masters of Smacks &c who are appointed to
command vessels to cruize on the coasts of Great
Britain are diligently to attend on board, and to
keep their vessels in constant motion*

(17th Century Customs House Order)

Up to the end of the 17th century, Customs House hired
small smacks which, sometimes helped by the Royal Navy,
were used as a kind of marine police force to keep an eye on
the owlers, if for nothing much besides. By 1698 export
smuggling increased in volume so much that the economic loss
became intolerable; the Royal Navy was accordingly required
to provide three men-of-war and four armed sloops to patrol
between the North Foreland and the Isle of Wight with orders
to board any vessel suspected of 'carrying wool or bringing any
goods or any suspected persons'. In addition, fourteen
Customs sloops, smacks, cutters or cruisers (the terms in this
context were interchangeable) were deployed around the
coast. Each of these (the largest about 200 tons) carried a
master, a mate and around 30 men; a distinctive identification
was flown, 'a jack and red ensign with the seal of office (a
castellated portcullis) thereon'. Masters were directed to 'speak
with all ships and vessels they shall meet at sea' and, if
smuggling were suspected, to 'diligently watch their motions
and keep them company until they are clear of the coast.' In
time of war, these Customs sloops were liable to be taken over
by the Royal Navy; life aboard, whether in peace or war, was
hard. Officially, the vessels were not permitted to enter
harbour except for essential repairs or for shelter in the
severest weather, but in practice it appears that some Masters
did not interpret these orders particularly strictly as a
complaint dated March 1747 to the Customs Commissioners
would suggest; not a single Customs sloop had been seen
cruising between Sandwich and Reculver for some months and

the Thanet smugglers were taking full advantage of this lamentable slackness.

Pay was hardly generous with a Master paid £1 weekly, a mate 14/- and a crew member 7/- plus an allowance for victuals of 9d daily 'whereof a notice is to be affixed to the Mast that if good & sufficient provisions are not provided by the Commander, the Mariners may complain.'

Uniform was adopted in 1777, when the masters and mates took on a naval-type rig (the first set of silver buttons supplied free) but epaulettes were not allowed because of the danger of confusion with the officers of the Royal Navy. One might have thought that, having been ordered to co-operate with Customs in their campaign against smuggling, the last-mentioned gentlemen would have been above reproach, but such was regrettably not always the case. In 1720, *HMS Bideford* (Capt Gregory) escorted George I across the Channel at the beginning of a state visit to Hanover. With his monarch safely deposited on dry land, Capt Gregory's official duties were over but, seizing a golden opportunity, he took the ship's pinnace

Shakespeare Cliff, Dover. Painted by Sam Atkins 1811.
A frigate (left background) with various large craft in the distance, the nearest could be an East Indiaman. The fishermen in the lugger and rowing boats (foreground) would be closely watching the movements of both.

into Rotterdam whence it returned to *Bideford* loaded to the gunwhales with first quality brandy, naturally as medical stores. Later that same year, Gregory took a trip down the Channel to meet up with the *Queen of Peace* an East Indiaman homeward bound off Beachy Head; taking aboard tea, chintzes, muslin and spirits he proceeded to run them ashore on the Kent coast. A favourite practice of his when lying off Deal was to grapple for tubs of brandy which had been previously sunk at known locations by smugglers who had already paid him to bring the spirits into port under the white ensign.

By 1784, the Waterguard strength had increased to 44 vessels of various sizes which were manned by a total of over 1,000 personnel; there were 20 more smacks hired from private owners. In that year, running costs were £44,355.16.11. One of the largest, *Tartar* of Dover (194 tons) accounted•for £1,304.6.2½, while the smallest, *Nimble* of Deal (41 tons) but carrying only one man less (30) recorded £1,064.9.9. The performance of the privately owned vessels was so abysmal that in 1788 the charter scheme was abandoned and the strength of the remainder, now on full establishment, was cut to 37, one of these was *HMS Vigilant* 82 tons, 8 guns, cruising off the Essex, Kent and Sussex coasts.

In many accounts of Customs activity at this time one encounters terms which, describing the various craft employed, may cause some confusion in the mind of the landsman. One hopes that the following list may elucidate the position: *Cruiser/Cruizer* Any ship detached from the main fleet for independent work such as reconnaissance or anti-smuggling duties. 'A superior and speedy type of craft' being called for, a frigate was often employed in this capacity.

Cutter/Sloop These terms were (late 18th century) often interchangeable although not strictly synonymous (see p.85). Smaller than a frigate and differently (fore-and-aft or yacht) rigged (see p.37), they were often used in the Royal Navy as auxiliary vessels and on revenue duties.

A 'gate' leading down to the sea. (see p.21)(Old print)

Broadstairs Fort converted into the Preventive Station in 1816, it overlooks the Bay to the front of Bleak House which, immortalised by Dickens, is now a Museum full of his possessions arranged as they were in his day. Maritime and smuggling relics are also featured in a separate part of the house. (Old print)

Frigate A warship with 'relatively little sheer to the hull', i.e. low in the water and often with one gun deck only. Three-masted and ship-rigged (see p.37) a frigate was small, fast and manoeuvrable; it was not used to fight in the line of battle but was reserved for fast scouting, message carrying and anti-smuggling patrols.

Lugger The favourite larger smuggling vessel, also used in the Royal Navy and Revenue service. Typically, it carried three masts, each with a lug-sail, but the renowned Deal lugger, much favoured for 'hovelling' (loitering off-shore as if waiting for haulage work, but sometimes with nefarious intent) was a variant which discarded the mainmast and sail.

Most Customs craft were armed, the favourite piece being the 6 pounder cannon of which as many as twelve might be carried; each required three men to serve it. A three pound charge of powder could hurl the ball a maximun of one mile, although the optimum range was 300 yards. The newly invented carronade was also employed; all guns were painted according to the captain's wishes. Often they were black all over with the brasswork polished, often dark grey with a scarlet band round the muzzle was favoured; other captains preferred a pure white.

A fine description of an early 19th century Revenue cutter is given by the writer of Victorian boys' adventure stories, Captain Frederick Marryat RN and as he commanded one, who better to write about it?:

'She is a cutter and you may know that she belongs to the Preventive Service by the number of gigs and galleys which she has hoisted up all round her. She looks like a vessel that is about to sail with a cargo of boats: two on deck, one astern, one each side of her. You observe that she is painted black and her bulwarks are painted red; it is not a very becoming colour but then, it lasts a long while, and the dockyard is not very generous on the score of paint—or lieutenants of the navy troubled with much spare cash. She has plenty of men, and fine men they all

A carronade often carried on a revenue cutter, first produced at Carron, Scotland, in 1779. Made in lengths from 2′ to 5′, it was lighter than the standard cannon but at close range far more destructive. It was manned by a crew of four; the opening shot at Trafalgar is said to have been fired by a 68pdr carronade, causing 400 casualties aboard the French Flagship *Bucentaure*. It had several defects, the most serious being its violent recoil which sometimes split the carriage and dismounted the gun. In 1980, two of these pieces were discovered by Messrs Lapthorne and Perkins working on the remains of a sunken wreck at Ramsgate harbour mouth which turned out to be the first Revenue craft ever recovered.

A Preventiveman aboard a Revenue cutter (Carronade on left). A contemporary watercolour.

are; dressed in red flannel shirts and blue trousers; some of them have not taken off their canvas or tarpaulin petticoats, which are very useful to them, as they are in the boats night and day, in all weathers. But we will at once go down into the cabin, where we shall find the lieutenant who commands her, a master's mate and a midshipman. They have each their tumbler before them and are drinking gin-toddy, hot with sugar—capital gin too, 'bove proof; it is from that small anker standing under the table. It is one that they forgot to return to the Custom House when they made their last seizure.'

Marryat turns an ironic eye upon the midshipman:

'He has been turned out of half the ships in the service for laziness, but he was born so and therefore it is not his fault. A Revenue cutter suits him—she is half the time hove-to; and he has no objection to boat-service, as he sits down in the stern-sheets, which is not fatiguing. Creeping for tubs is his delight, as he gets over so little ground.'

Contemporary legal authorities were by no means unanimous in defining the exact difference between a sloop and a cutter. Expert evidence quoted by a judge in one case brought by the Crown did not exactly clarify the position:

'The difference between a sloop and a cutter is as follows, a standing or running bowsprit is common to either and a traveller is an invariable portion of a cutter's rig, as is a jib-tack. The jib-sheet differs, that of a cutter is twice as large as that of a sloop and is differently set without a stay whereas a sloop's jib-sheet is set with a fixed stay. Furthermore, in a cutter, the tack of the jib is hooked to a traveller and there is a large thimble fastened to a block which comes across the head of the sail, there being two blocks at the head of the mast, one on each side. A rope passes through the three blocks, by which it is drawn up to the halliards. The jib of a cutter lets down and draws in a very short time, moreover a cutter usually has channels and mortice-holes to prevent over-setting.'

Another authority (E. K. Chatterton, *King's Cutters and Smugglers*) puts the matter rather more succinctly: 'Practically, sloops and cutters of those days were one and the same, with very minor differences.'

The Waterguard was administered in a highly complicated fashion by no fewer than six separate authorities, giving rise to frequent confusion and occasional ill-feeling:

'Between the English Customs cruisers and the English Excise cruisers there was as much friendship as usually exists between a dog and a cat . . . similarly, between the Custom House and the Naval vessels there was considerable jealousy and every display of that pompous, bombastic exhibition of character which was such a feature of life in the 18th and early 19th centuries' *(King's Cutters and Smugglers).*

The Preventive Waterguard

Not a disciplined force, often in league with the smugglers.

(Capt W. McCulloch RN)

Despite these strictures, uttered by the commander of a rival force and perhaps not entirely unbiased, the establishment of the Preventive Waterguard in 1809 was at least some attempt at plugging the gap between the revenue cruisers far out to sea and the riding officers on the coastal strip which was becoming so painfully and expensively manifest.

With the entire mainland coast divided into three, Kent was placed in the London-Land's End sector which had been allocated 23 cutters and 42 rowing boats. The force was confined to coastal waters and when prevented by rough weather from taking to the sea, crews were required to patrol the shore on foot. Most of the personnel were ex-navy men paid with a retainer of £5 per annum plus 3/- daily when actually employed—not especially attractive for a life both dangerous and uncomfortable, although there was always the chance of a bonus for recovering contraband and capturing smugglers. The 'preventive man' was stationed as far away from his native heath as possible in order to discourage collusion with local men, but this practice also gave rise to accommodation problems as few villagers were prepared to board and lodge someone who was threatening the main local industry. In an attempt to circumvent this difficulty the building of watch-houses incorporating living-quarters was considered but this manoeuvre was often countered by the reluctance of local landowners—no doubt swayed by local opinion—to sell the government suitable building sites. Compulsory purchase was resorted to, but where there was no alternative the luckless crews were forced to shelter in tents, or even under sails and tarpaulins, in the most miserable conditions. By 1817, considerable reform and re-organisation at least ensured that each boat was properly equipped with:

'One small flat cask holding two gallons of fresh water, one small water-tight cask to hold provisions, one chest of arms and ammunition, one Custom House jack, two spying-glasses (one for the watch-house the other for the boat), one small bucket for baling, one 'wall-piece' and 40 cartridges, thirty muskets or carbines, twenty light pistols and balls in proportion, bayonets, cutlasses, pouches, tucks, small hand hatchets for cutting away rigging, musket and pistol flints, cleaning materials, one set of rummaging tools and one dark lanthorn.'

The 'wall-piece' mentioned was a short, heavy musketoon throwing a large ball weighing close on ½lb; it had a kick like a mule but was highly effective at repelling boarders. The muskets were muzzle-loading flint-locks, smooth-bored with an effective range of 100 yards, the bullet weighing between one and two ounces. The cutlass was a fearsome curved heavy sword, fully a yard long and a favoured weapon throughout the Navy. Rummaging tools were those used in searching for contraband; such items as saws, chisels and axes were

87

included, besides the long iron rods or 'prickers' which were thrust into bales and the like when searching for contraband. Gradually the force became accepted and as it settled into its routine new responsibilities were added from time to time; by 1819 ship-wreck stations had been established under the Preventive Waterguard's jurisdiction, equipped with Manby mortars for firing life-lines to ships in distress (the inventor was one of Nelson's boyhood friends). By that same year too rations were improved (on paper at least) the daily allowance being a pound and a half each of bread and meat and half a gallon of beer together with vegetables, flour and cheese as and when available. A medicine chest too was installed in each boat to contain *inter alia* 'vomitting powders, purging powders, sweating and fever powders, calomel pills, laudanum *(or opium, for relief of severe pain)*, cough drops, stomach tincture, bark for the diarrhoea, scurvy drops, smelling salts of hartshorn peppermint, friar's balsam, basilicon 'for the healing of sluggish ulcers', mercurial ointment, blistering ointment, sticking plaster and lint.' Medical instruction was to be given and directions posted on how to apply a tourniquet 'which is to stop a violent bleeding from a wounded artery in the limbs till it can be properly secured and tied by a surgeon'.

Revenue Cutters stationed in Kent, 1784

Name	Crew	Station	Remarks
Defence	16	Gravesend	On the Establishment
Success	23	Rochester	On the Establishment
Otter	13	Rochester	Moored in Stangate Creek guarding the Quarantine station
Active	18	Faversham	On the Establishment
Sprightly	30	Sandwich	Employed on Contract
Scourge	30	Deal	Employed on Contract
Nimble	30	Deal	Employed on Contract
Tartar	31	Dover	On the Establishment
Assistance	28	Dover	Employed on Contract
Alert	16	Dover	Employed on Contract

Revenue Cutters stationed in Kent, 1797

Name	Crew	Tons	Guns	Commander	Cruising stations
Vigilant	?	82	8	Richd Dozell	Essex, Kent, Sussex coasts (winter only)
Defence	18	76	6	Geo Farr (actg)	Gravesend-Dungeness
Ant	15	58	4	Thos Morris	Gravesend-Nore
Fly	15	52	4	Thos Gibbs	Gravesend-Nore
Success	24	74	6	Wm Broadbank	Rochester — North Sand Head
Otter	13	68	?	Jno Matthews	Rochester-Woolpack Buoy
Active	18	75	8	Thos Lesser	Mouth of Medway-North Foreland, round the Longsand and up the Swin to Leigh
Swift	8	52	?	J. Westbeech	Downes to the Longsand
Nimble	15	41	2	Wm Clothier (actg)	Between the Forelands
Tartar	23	100	10	B. J. Worthington	The Gore to Beachy Head
Stag	32	153	14	Jno Haddock	Dover-Brighton, extended in special circumstances
Hound	30	111	12	J. R. Hawkins	North Foreland-Isle of Wight

In 1825, further dietary improvements were inaugurated; daily rations should by now have been: Biscuit and beef, 1lb of each, Rum (pure West Indian at least one year old) ¼ pint but to be diluted 1:3 parts water before issuing, Flour ½lb, Suet ¼lb (alternating with 1½oz sugar or ¼oz tea), Cabbage 1lb or Barley 2oz. It is interesting to note here an extract from the proceedings of a symposium *Starving Sailors* held at Greenwich (1980)—'Information as to what was actually consumed is more difficult to obtain but it is certain that the depredations of pursers, rats, weevils and inadequate storage meant that the sailors received far less than their official allowance.' Although these observations referred specifically to Nelson's sailors, there is no reason to doubt that human nature at least had much changed over the ensuing twenty years.

A horrid, bad station . . . nothing but wrecks all over the coast (Nelson).

(Old print)

The Coast Blockade

*Seamen or petty officers of men-of-war rarely enter.
The roll is thus filled for the most part by 'waisters'
("men strong enough but too stupid to be stationed
aloft") from discharged crews or, which is more
frequent, by unskilled though hardy Irish landsmen
whose estrangement from the sentiments, habits
and religion of those placed under their surveillance
seems to point them out as particularly adapted for
a service whose basis consists in an insidious
watchfulness over others and a hostile segregation
from their fellow men.*

Capt W. Glascock RN
A Naval Sketchbook Series 1, 1832

The Royal Naval Coast Blockade for the Prevention of
Smuggling had its origins in another blockade, that of the
French ports of the English Channel in the Napoleonic Wars.
Using the experience gained then, Captain Thomas Renwick
RN submitted his plans for a similar operation against the
smugglers, centred upon the coasts of Kent and Sussex.
Renwick however appears to have faded into the background
for it is the name of 'Flogging Joey', as Captain William
McCulloch was known (behind his back) to all who came into
contact with him, that is usually associated with the Blockade's
operation.

William McCulloch (1782-1825) spent most of his life in the
Royal Navy; third son of the Laird of Barholm,
Kircudbrightshire, he enlisted as midshipman in 1798; much
of his early service was spent blockading the French channel
ports. At 32 he was appointed to command the newly-
commissioned frigate *Barosa* on the Leeward Islands station;
two years later he was posted to another frigate *Ganymede* on
anti-smuggling patrols off the Kent coast. Here and then
commenced the work for which he is still remembered.

The avowed objective of the Blockade's commander was

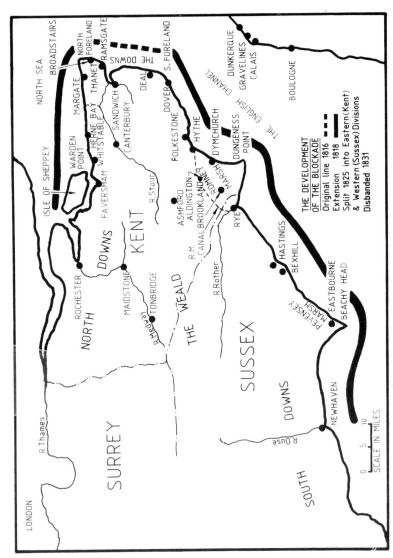

The Development of the Coast Blockade.

magnificent in its simplicity — 'to make the grass grow in the streets of Deal'; in other words the gangs were to be wiped off the face of the earth. No respite was to be given, the smuggler was to be hunted and challenged wherever and whenever he was encountered.

The first move was to blockade the stretch of coast between the North and South Forelands, this to be accomplished by boat patrols rowed out from *Ganymede* then stationed in the Downs, 'pending the development of more efficacious measures'. The men were put ashore at sunset, they patrolled the cliff tops and beaches all night and were withdrawn at daybreak. This in itself appears a Herculean task, coupled with the notoriously bad weather often experienced in that stretch of the Channel (the Downs were described by Nelson as 'a horrid, bad station, such weather I never saw in my life, nothing but wrecks all over the coast'), it must perhaps have daunted even the Royal Navy. At any rate, plans were soon changed and the Blockade came ashore more permanently with 'a complete cordon of sentinels posted within hailing distance of each other along the entire coast of Kent and Sussex on the brink of the tide'. The much-derided Martello towers — 'Pitt's Follies' built against an invasion that never happened — were at last to prove their worth as much needed accommodation for the patrols, and new watch-houses were built where required. To ensure constant vigilance the sentries were visited frequently by an officer and changed at irregular intervals; discipline, with the force under Admiralty and not Customs control, was as strict as on any naval vessel. *Ganymede* was replaced by *Severn*, another frigate; she was later joined by *Ramillies*, a third-rate man-of-war. The number of men on the books of both was 'considerably swollen to meet the requirements of the new scheme' giving a total strength of 1,300. In the shore establishments (each land station was commanded by a lieutenant) the flavour of life was distinctly that of the sea-going navy. The men lived in 'long-rooms' and slept in hammocks; married quarters of a sort were

Sandgate Castle (Old print, Folkestone Library). Reproduced by kind permission. Built by Henry VIII, modernised in 1805 to form part of the anti-invasion scheme, along with the Martello towers and the Royal Military Canal. In 1816 it was occupied by the Coast Blockade.

available when part of the long-room was screened off 'where the men and their families enjoyed such privacy as a strip of Navy canvas could afford'. Brutal discipline was the order of the day — even the Royal Navy thought so — with Flogging Joey earning his soubriquet by his practice of 'driving his men to their duty like a Mediterranean slave-master with the cat at their backs'. Opinions vary as to the Blockade's worth and efficiency but it is undeniable that it made its presence felt and that within a year of its establishment the Preventive Waterguard was withdrawn from Kent and Sussex, leaving the smugglers to the tender mercy of Flogging Joey and his Warriors. Soon the whole coast was up in arms against them, fulminating against 'base tools of a despotic government'; a Blockade patrol on the Deal-St Margaret's Bay road was attacked by a mob, its leader shouting, 'You damned infernal rascals, if it weren't for you I should be a rich man by now!' The more prudent Traders withdrew leaving the action to those who had decided that their only chance of survival was to combine in a determined effort to break the ring of steel which

One of 'Pitt's Follies'.
Close on two hundred years later it still defies the onslaught of time.

A Lieutenant of the Royal Navy
(1799).
Drawn by Rowlandson; many were
later employed in the Coast
Blockade. There were close on
4,000 on the Navy List for 1819.

The Coast Blockade 'warriors' and, later, the 'beach trampers' of the Preventive
Waterguard were fair game for cartoonists. *Punch* was particularly scathing. (see
p.98)

was slowly encircling them. Thus it was that coastal Kent and Sussex came to suffer those frequent bloody affrays in which so many on both sides were to die. Surgeons' reports make gruesome reading but they certainly emphasise the courage and suffering of those concerned. One 'incorrigible smuggler', Hogben, had his thigh smashed by a pistol ball in an encounter with the Blockade near Folkestone in April 1820 'on which occasion he was considered to be, if not mortally wounded, so much disabled as to be incapable of further mischief'. In view of this, he was placed in the care of some Folkestone surgeons who promised that he would be produced as and when required. Having quickly regained the use of his leg, he absconded to rejoin the Blues.

Towards the end of its fifteen years of existence, morale within the Force sank lower and lower; the harsh discipline, the irksome duties, the constant threat of death or maiming,

The 'Preventive' water-guard or coastguard. A caricature of 1833.

all caused recruiting problems, and, besides this, problems within the service itself became increasingly manifest. With bribery and corruption rampant, the men started to lose the will to win, and many cases of self-mutilation (to obtain discharge) were reported. With the armed smuggler to their front and with the 'cat' to their behind, small wonder indeed that they often chose to come to terms with their adversaries. By 1831 it was time to call it a day and the Coast Blockade was abolished 'without a single tear shed for its demise'. It was the turn of the newly reformed Coast Guard to try its teeth on the 'midnight men of Kent'.

The Coast Guard

Castles of idleness where able-bodied men spend their time in looking through long glasses for imaginary smugglers.

'Punch's' opinion of the behaviour of the Coast Guards in their newly completed stations was a completely unfair one for, in truth, the work was long and arduous and the discipline and traditions strictly naval.

The new Coast Guard — the two words were not united until some years after its inception — was descended from the Preventive Waterguard which it superceded in 1821; it also took over the functions and responsibilities of the revenue cruisers and the riding officers and was thus the principle anti-smuggling force. Controlled by the Customs, only the Royal Naval Coast Blockade operating on the south-east coast was outside its remit and, with the abolition of that force in 1831 it became the one and only authority to deal with the Traders, although it could still call upon the military for assistance if required and it was also possible to utilise another newly formed organisation — the Bow Street Runners.

In this year too the Royal Navy's influence increased considerably; in terminology, in dress and in drill the Admiralty flavour was unmistakable and so, in the uniform if nothing else, it remains today. Under the new regime the division of the force into sea-going and land establishments was more strongly emphasised; recruits to the marine branch were required to serve in naval ships abroad if called upon to do so and training was given at naval stations; thus a reserve for the Royal Navy was brought into being, which was to prove its worth in the Crimean War over twenty years later. The Land Section (once the Landguard of Riding Officers) underwent yet another metamorphosis to emerge as the Mounted Guard. All the old men (see p.78) were compulsorily retired and the fresh entrants had to be 20-30 years old with previous experience in a cavalry regiment. The lower ranks adopted army nomenclature up to the rank of sergeant, but the pay was decidedly more attractive with a private starting at 4/- daily plus an initial grant of £50 to buy his own horse and saddlery; the horse's meals were paid for by the government

An old-time Coast Guard

COAST GUARD CERTIFICATE OF SERVICE,—to be granted to Chief Boatmen, Commissioned Boatmen, Boatmen and Mounted Guard; in every case of removal or discharge.

Name of Party _James Smith_   Rank _Boatman_
(at full length)
Station _Walmer_   Port _Deal_

Date of Original Entry into the Service	Date of Appearance at the above Station	Date of Discharge	Cause of Discharge	Character and general Conduct
6 hours 1845	11th April 1846	30th Sept. 1847	As the joined of the Service	Steady man and keeps a vigilant look out.

* This Column to be filled up (after full consideration) with the strictest impartiality.

Approved _____ Chief Officer
_____ Inspecting Commander.

No. 16, Coast Guard.—Certificates of Service.   *(turn over)* 18—9

Compl. Fau. No 3277.

A Certificate of Service.

James Smith, born 1818 in Aberdeen, was domiciled in Deal. Having served five years as a 'Mariner' on HM Revenue Cruisers *Cheerful* and *Camelion,* he joined the revenue Coast Guard Service, as it was then called, as a Probationary Boatman in 1845 and retired (1875) as a Commissioned Boatman, living to draw his pension until well into the 20th century. Besides service at Walmer and Deal, he was stationed at Stiffkey (Norfolk), Newgate (Sussex), Southampton and Pembroke (Wales). He was seconded for service to the Royal Navy for two years as an AB in *HMS Princess Royal,* for which he received the Baltic and the Crimean campaign medals. (Document loaned and information kindly supplied by a great-grandson of James Smith, Mr. Tom Lilly of Kingsdown, Deal who is himself ex Royal Navy (CPO, regular)

100

also. Personal arms were government issue, a cavalry pattern sabre and two pistols and the uniform too was supplied. This was blue with gilt buttons inscribed with an anchor encircled by the words *Coast Guard*. A great-coat similar in pattern to that of the newly formed Police force comprised part of the *ensemble* which was topped off by a round glazed black hat in naval style encircled by a ribbon again bearing the legend *HM Coast Guard*. The higher echelons, comprising some fifty Commanders and two Captains RN, retained their naval ranks and rates of pay. Concurrent with all these reforms, it was mooted by some that more off-duty amenities should be provided for the ratings, including 'libraries of books of an entertaining and moral tendency.' One person in favour of this move was the famous social worker the Quaker Mrs Fry; this gave 'Anon' the excuse for the following stanza:

> Quoth that excellent dame, Mrs Fry,
> "The life of our Coast Guards is dry!"
> So she sent them good books
> On the downfall of crooks
> And the ghastly results of a lie
>
> The Coast Guards, whose minds required feeding
> With novels of taste and good breeding
> Turned over the pages
> By slow painful stages
> Then from Cornwall to Kent gave up reading.

The fact that the Blockade had withdrawn did not signify that peace had come to reign over our southern shores; on the contrary the Coast Guard was to find its hands full. In his first year, the commandant of the Folkestone district issued orders that muskets were to be loaded with condemned ball which presumably had greater spread and stopping power although possibly it was in the interests of economy. The men were also again economically advised to 'provide themselves with stout

101

Weavers' cottages.
These buildings in the Weald (see p.21) had high gables and large windows to give as much room and admit as much light as possible.
Names are gone—what men they were
these their cottages declare. (Edmund Blunden)

Boughton Monchelsea Place, Kent.
The Kentish wool trade, inextricably mixed with owling, enabled many a Kentish gentleman to live comfortably in such establishments.
This Tudor dwelling stands on the site of a mediaeval manor house.

hats of sufficient substance to protect the head from a common bat'. Presumably the commander did not have anti-rabies precautions in mind and the 'bat' referred to was a blow from the cudgel of a 'batsman'. Additional instructions were to keep their cutlasses sharp and to have them fitted with a strap so that they could not be knocked out of the hand.

Many of the naval lieutenants in charge of the Kent stations were nearing the end of their service and feeling a little leg-weary were perhaps inclined to take things easily, if they could; a simple labour-saving scheme however, attracted displeasure from on high:

'Deal, 9th October 1831. Having on a recent night visit observed an officer under my command riding a donkey on the beach to visit his guards, instead of using every precaution to keep his situation as much as possible from the smugglers, as well as from his crew, I desire that this practice be discontinued, assuring the officer alluded to that I shall not keep such idleness from the Comptroller General.'

Donkeys seem to have specialised in attracting official disapproval by over-eating and behaving in other anti-social ways:

'Folkestone, January 1839. The Board have expressed disapprobation at the amount charged for forage for donkeys in this District; in their opinion the purchase of beans is wholly unnecessary and too many oats have been given . . .'

In June 1837, the Board ordained that the donkey stationed at No 27 Tower (one of the pair guarding the Globsden Gut sluice gates opposite St Mary's church south of Dymchurch) to be disposed of by exchanging it with the one at Lydd,

'complaints having reached me regarding his vicious habits. As soon as the exchange has taken place, the commanding boatman at No 27 Tower will sell the Lydd donkey by public auction.'

No doubt the new technique of controlling the smuggler by

constant presence of vigilant personnel rather than by simply chasing and blazing away at him was starting to pay dividends and yet on the other hand, it is undeniable that the major cause of decline in smuggling was economic; the Free Trade policies brought in by Peel and Gladstone later in the century either abolished or so reduced the import duties on tea, wine and spirits that eventually tobacco remained as the only worthwhile proposition — until some clever fellow thought of Swiss watches.

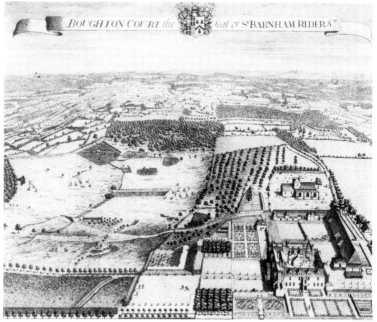

Badslade's View (south) from Boughton Monchelsea Place (early 18c).
What are those blue remembered hills,
What spires, what farms are those? (A.E. Housman)
Answer: All good smuggling country. Many places in this panorama can still be identified; e.g. Goudhurst church, famous for its part in the rout of the Hawkhurst gang (1747) in mid-distance to the right. To the left is flat country leading down into Romney Marsh.

The Law and the Smuggler

Every prosecution out of the Customs House is looked upon as a tyrannical way of proceeding, little less than an invasion of property and, by the Exchequer jurors and judges, the poor Merchants are the favourites.

(Roger North KC, 1680)

As this quotation shows, the popular concept that the face of the law was set firm against the smugglers was not always the case in hard practice. This impression is reinforced by an essay by Joseph Trevers published in 1675.

To the Restoring of our Decayed Trade:

'It is well known that smugglers are not of the meanest persons in the places where they dwell, but oftentimes have great interest with the magistrates and, being purse-proud, do not value what they spend to ingratiate themselves with persons of authority, by bribes to stop their mouths.'

The Kentish owler was so well organised that time and time again he flouted the anti-smuggling laws with impunity; even when caught in the act he often got away scot-free with a little help from 'persons in authority'. When a case brought by the Customs commissioners did get to court, strict proof was always called for; circumstantial evidence counted for very little. Sir Thomas Hardress KC, MP for Canterbury towards the end of the 17th century was well aware of this fact; in the Court of Exchequer (where the major smuggling cases were heard) he was affectionately known as 'The Smuggler's

105

Friend'. With his encyclopaedic knowledge of Customs law allied with an equally extensive acquaintance with the Holy Scripture, it was his favourite ploy to exhaust the prosecution, and doubtless the judge also, with long drawn-out histrionic appeals to the Laws of God and Nature. Sir Thomas was seldom short of a brief for in those days his constituency was infested by owlers, mainly 'sturdy young fellows' who lodged with the Walloon weavers who had settled in Canterbury having escaped from religious persecution in their native land.

The efforts of the few in authority who did attempt to curb owling were in the main of little avail and the passing of a law in 1662 making the smuggling of wool a crime punishable by death seems only to have encouraged the practitioners in the belief that they might as well be hung for a sheep as a lamb; abandoning the bludgeon in favour of the pistol and musket they proceeded much as before. After some thirty years the death penalty was rescinded and at the same time more

The Customs House. London, in mediaeval times. By Christopher Hughes.

stringent regulations brought in regarding the transport of wool near the coasts of Kent and Sussex. The owlers' reaction to new legislation can be just as well imagined as described.

The law-makers of the early 18th century turned their attention to the type of vessel employed in the Trade with restrictions placed upon light craft even those engaged in ostensibly law-abiding commerce. The ownership of small fast ships and of roomy open boats—both types widely used in

A Reward Poster (1832) offering 'Blood money'. (see p.109)

smuggling — was allowed to private individuals only but efforts in this direction were largely to be frustrated by 'those legal luminaries ignorant of shipping' who had the task of drafting the various Bills. A classic example was in the definition of a cutter (see p.85); it was quite wrongly assumed that this term would be universally accepted and the fact that the terminology of boat-building varies from port to port was quite overlooked. It took the Solicitor General thirty years to produce a legally acceptable definition and in that interval full advantage was taken of the loophole so fortuitously offered. The case of the *Joseph*, a Dover built vessel putting into Cowes in June 1788, clearly demonstrates how well the smugglers could argue their point. The Collector of Customs at that port (William Arnold, father of the celebrated Dr Arnold, head of Rugby school and immortalised in *Tom Brown's Schooldays*) seized the craft on the suspicion that she was intending to intercept homeward-bound East Indiamen to take off contraband tea. The Master replied that he was breaking no law, that he was engaged in piloting and that in any case as the *Joseph* was not a decked vessel she ought to be classified as a boat and consequently outside the law under which he was detained. Countering this argument, Arnold cited the opinions of a Cowes cutter builder and the local Revenue commander that she should definitely be regarded as a lugger or a sloop for 'it is absurd to consider the vessel a boat when she tows at her stern, or carries on board, a boat 17′ long and 5′2″ wide'.

The operators of pleasure boats had to operate under a special licence from the Admiralty; long delay in issuing these and their high cost gave great cause for complaint.

A heaven-sent opportunity to evade the law was seized as soon as it was realised that the new Acts exempted the fishing-boat from registration — simply take on a sufficiency of nets and other gear and you were free to practise the Wicked Trade with impunity!

Various other penalties were brought in throughout the

century; in 1717 the new price for owling was transportation to the Americas and some nineteen years later the 'Smugglers' Act' reintroduced the death penalty in the shape of 'hanging without benefit of clergy' for wounding, or even merely obstructing, 'by force of arms' a Revenue officer in the course of his duty. The same Act provided for a reward of £50 and a free pardon to any smuggler who betrayed his mates—this became known as 'blood money'. Loitering within five miles of the coast was prohibited and collective fines were introduced whereby the county in which the offence occurred was fined £200, to be remitted if the culprits were discovered and apprehended within six months. Remission of sentence could be earned by enlistment into the Royal Navy but, although the smuggler was always highly regarded therein (see p.41) he would usually avoid the King's service at all costs and, if impressed, would contrive to desert to be back at his old Trade within weeks. An ingenious enlistment scheme was tried out in 1778 by which a jailed smuggler could win his freedom by producing two recruits for the Navy but rather predictably there is not a single record of any enlistments made by this method. Draconian measures were taken by an Act of 1805 *For the more effectual Prevention of Smuggling* which directed that any physically fit seaman found aboard any vessel whose build, rig, cargo, registration, position or behaviour rendered her liable to seizure, was to be deemed a smuggler by association, even when no contraband was found to be carried. The automatic punishment of impressment into the Navy for five years (to be extended in time of war) without appearing before a magistrate exempted only those medically unfit; it underlines the precarious manpower position of Nelson's navy. Hundreds of smugglers were netted annually by this Act. They were taken to a major naval base such as Portsmouth, to be held there for one month allowing time for legal redress and release in the few cases where a man was proved to have been merely an innocent passenger. The newly impressed seaman was then posted to any ship bound for foreign waters; when the ship was due to return home the smuggler was transferred to another until his term was completed; there is on record the case of one man who, having come to the end of his five year stretch on Christmas Day in mid-ocean, refused to serve the King one moment more. His subsequent court-martial exonerated him and he was released forthwith. Some smugglers distinguished themselves so well in their Naval service, for example at the bombardment of Algiers (1816) and at the Battle of Navarino (1827) that they

*Pye Alley Farm
—still standing (just).*
(see p.116)

were recommended for, and in some cases were given, their early discharge. For a most interesting account of an impressed smuggler who fought at Navarino, the reader is referred to the article *A Smuggler's Medal* by Capt K. J. Douglas-Morris RN in the *Journal* of the Orders and Medals Research Society, No. 3 1981.

In 1779, boats with six (or, in the case of Kent, four) oars were declared illegal but this had little effect on the livelihood of the galley builders of Deal, Dover and Folkestone many of whom crossed over to France to carry on their work in Calais (see p.119) Yet another blow against the Trade at that time was

Bounds Brook, Convicts' Wood. (see p.116)

the decree that any craft taken smuggling was to be sawn into three and then broken up; Pitt the Younger was the sworn enemy of the smugglers in those days and is most remembered in Deal for his action there (see p.70).

Woe betide the attorney who as well as numbering supporters of the Trade among his clients was also instrumental in bringing about smugglers' arrests! Such was the unfortunate predicament of Mr Boys, Clerk to the Margate Bench who was closely involved in the arrest and conviction of nineteen members of the North Kent gang in 1823:

> 'Mr Boys was the object of almost general hatred in the town of Margate; he was placarded on the walls as an informer and hunter after blood-money, his house was frequently assailed, his windows broken and his person assaulted in the dark, the fruit trees in his garden destroyed in the night . . . ' (Reported by the Crown solicitor.)

Swalecliffe Rock. (see p.116)

A Profitable Sideline

The English smugglers are a likeable people and have courage and the ability to do anything for money . . . they are a terrible people.

(Napoleon Bonaparte)

The commodities which over the centuries attracted the attention and expertise of the Kentish smuggler were many and varied but none, surely, was as remarkable as that traffic in humans which was carried on out of Whitstable during the French wars (1793-1815) during which time thousands of prisoners were taken. The officers were often put on parole and billeted with private families; those less favoured were confined in hastily erected prisons—such as Princeton on Dartmoor, but the worst fate of all was to be confined in a hulk, an antiquated man-of-war which, no longer fit for service, had been stripped of all its fittings and dismasted and thus converted into a floating prison to be moored off Sheerness, Woolwich, Portsmouth or Plymouth. Once incarcerated here a prisoner's chances of escape were slim indeed, unless outside help could be enlisted—as it sometimes was from the Whitstable smugglers.

The fishermen of Whitstable were very well placed for this invisible export; their yawls and cutters plied regularly across to Flushing and to Ostend and, since we were not at war with the Netherlands, these routes could be used with impunity although, as already described, the mere fact of his country being at war did not influence the smuggler much in his choice of ports. First came the question of payment, a price had to be

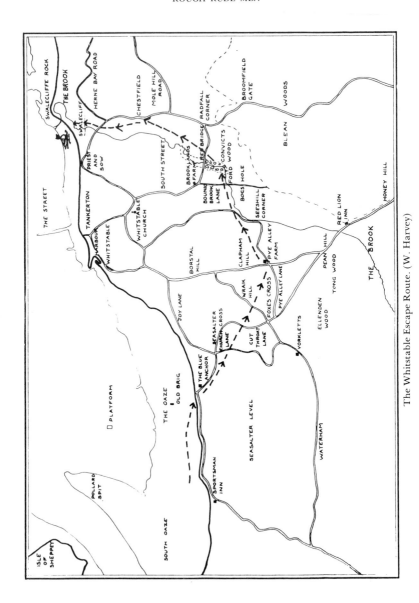

The Whitstable Escape Route. (W. Harvey)

An Imperial Visit to the Cellars 27th July 1807. (Old print)
Almost certainly some of Messrs Moet & Chandon's merchandise would find its
unofficial way from Epernay to Dover and thence to London. In 1834, Customs
calculated that 23 hogsheads, 4 casks, 13 cases, 24 bottles and 12 gallons of wine plus
50 bottles of liqueurs had been imported in the name of the French ambassador,
Talleyrand. This was twelve times the permitted quantity and gave Lord Palmerston
the Foreign Secretary cause to remark: *This seems an ENORMOUS quantity of wine
for one family.*

settled by various agents who would approach the prisoner's
family. This done, the prisoner was located — here bribes
would have played an important part — and word got to him as
to how and when he was to make his bid for freedom. Were he
rich enough, all transport would be paid for, otherwise the
fugitive was required to find his way to London or, if nearer,
to Whitstable. The luckier individual with his travel arranged
would be supplied with a post-chaise, travelling by day and
hiding up at night for rest and refreshment; on his arrival in
London, he would be slipped aboard one of the Whitstable
hoys (engaged for centuries in the coasting trade) or an oyster
boat plying daily from Billingsgate down the Thames to
Seasalter. Here, just by the Blue Anchor inn, the sea ebbs

some two miles exposing a vast expanse of firm sand; here stood a high platform where fishing boats would moor to unload their catch which was there and then gutted and packed; the resulting activity providing good cover for the escaping prisoners who could mix with the throng of everyday people going about their daily business. Here, then, they would lie low until under the cloak of darkness they essayed the next stage of their journey, a two mile trek across reedy dykes south-east to Pye Alley farm to meet up with Thomas Goodwin, a key member of the escape organisation who arranged food, shelter and rest. Then the party would make for Convicts' Wood where they might have to endure a wait of several weeks hidden away in the dense undergrowth until all was good and ready for the final dash to the sea. Here during their sojourn, supplies would be brought over from Bounds Brook (now Brooklands) farm and to while away the long waiting hours and to show gratitude to their hosts, perhaps even to earn a little money, the Frenchmen would make up little highly decorative boxes out of paper and straw, one at least of which has survived. At long last, the word would come through that all was ready; now came the time to follow Bogs Hole brook down to the sea by way of Chestfield thence on to the Old Fan inn where the Herne Bay road now crosses the brook. At this point, rations for the sea voyage would be given out, then it was back again to the brook to follow it down to the sea to Swalecliffe Rock, then a high bank of shingle which has since those days suffered considerable erosion. In the lee of this bank the escaping French would take their last look at England for there in front of them drawn up on the beach would be a dinghy waiting to ferry them out to a smuggling cutter hove-to in the shadows off-shore. Within hours, given reasonable fortune, their time of tribulation would be ended.

The Guinea Traders

All those men have their price.

(Sir Robert Walpole 1676-1745,
referring to so-called patriots)

During the Napoleonic wars, Deal, Dover, and Folkestone all attained a certain notoriety for their involvement in a highly specialised branch of the Trade, the smuggling of gold to an enemy country to pay enemy troops. Napoleon describes in his Memoirs how it was done:

'I got bills upon Vera Cruz which certain agents sent by circuitous routes by Amsterdam, Hamburg and other places, to London. The bills were discounted by London merchants to whom 10%, and sometimes a premium, was paid as their reward. Bills were then given by them upon different European bankers for the greater part of the amount, and the remainder in gold, which last was brought over to France by the smugglers. Even for equipping my last expedition *(i.e. Waterloo)* a great part of the money was raised in London.'

The good golden guinea was king of currency in those times and with the price of gold rocketting it was fetching 27/- in the street markets whence by devious routes it would find its way to one of the Kent ports mentioned. Here, in the company of several thousands of its fellows it would obtain temporary sanctuary in the house of the ordinary otherwise law-abiding citizen whose teapot, kettle and long-case clock made excellent caches. Soon, with utmost stealth and secrecy the coins would gravitate to the final collecting point — the sail loft on the

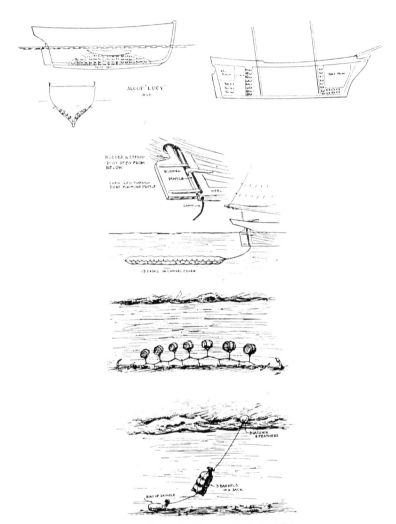

"Concealments" and methods of tub-sinking.

118

Stade at Folkestone was one such. Here all would be packed snug and secure into long leather purses to be secured round the smuggler's body for the Channel crossing which was often made in a 'guinea boat'. These giant galleys, forty feet long and seven feet wide were rowed by thirty-six stout oarsmen; it was forbidden by law to build such craft in England, consequently the English craftsmen crossed over to Calais where they were permitted to do so in peace, under licence from the French government, provided that a third of the crew were French. The cost of such a vessel was £40, not a lot to lose even on a maiden trip provided the guineas (value £30,000 a consignment) got safely through. These galleys were notoriously difficult to catch, as one Naval officer put it 'Sending a cutter after one of those was like sending a cow to catch a hare'.

Some Kentish Cleverness

> We smuggling boys are merry boys
> Sometimes here and sometimes there,
> No rent or taxes do we pay,
> But a man-o'-war is all our fear.
> (Anon *The Ballad of Dover Gaol* 1810)

A demonstrably first-class seaman, the Kentish sea-smuggler also possessed a vast repertoire of stratagems and low cunning by which he often outwitted his adversaries; his land equivalent also did not lack this expertise.

The vessels of the Honourable East India Company, the famous East Indiamen, homeward bound up-Channel, played a large part in fostering the Trade. Since Tudor times commerce with the East Indies had been steadily growing; by the early 1600s the trading posts had developed into companies, British, French, Dutch, Portuguese, Danish and

Swedish — all Europe was avid for 'sugar and spice and all things nice' to disguise the flavour of meat which by winter's end had long lost its pristine freshness. The Company's vessels evolved along with its growing trade. The proto-type East Indiaman was a pot-bellied galleon built for capacity rather than speed — 'the fat East Indiaman' which carried out to the Indies household goods, wines and watches, along with gold and silver, to return its holds stuffed and redolent with spices, sugar, opium, silk and ivory. As competition got fiercer, so the ships became more warlike, armed as men-of-war and quite capable of taking care of themselves if attacked, as indeed they often were. The Company's ships attacked their rivals with as much vigour and thrust as the Company men ashore pursued their Eastern associates; its sea-officers were top of their profession, the recognised *crème de la crème* of the shipping

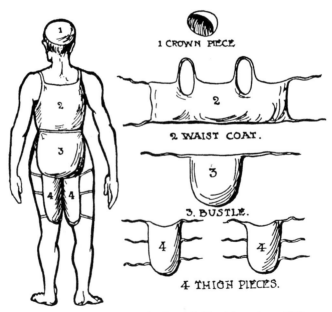

1 CROWN PIECE.

2 WAIST COAT.

3. BUSTLE.

4 THIGH PIECES.

How the Deal Boatmen used to Smuggle Tea Ashore. (see p.121)

120

world. This fact, however, did not deter every crew member, from the Captain down, from dabbling in the Trade. The bulk of smuggling was done when the homecoming vessel anchored safely in the Downs. Here the Deal boatmen would swarm out in their luggers and other small craft to purchase quantities of 'uncustomed' tea which obviously had to be got ashore undetected. This manoeuvre was often accomplished by the wearing of a special costume (see illustration); once ashore, the tea might be locally distributed to the grocer or direct to the housewife or it could have been handed over to the 'duffer' a most important link in the supply chain to London. With his specially designed coat taking 30lbs of tea in its lining, he would walk on up to London where it found a ready market.

Smuggling vessels themselves had ingeniously contrived

A galley
(Deal Museum).

121

hiding places built-in, called 'concealments'; the *Mary* of Dover was only 14′ long and less than 6′ wide yet she was fitted with a double bottom and false sides taking thirty tin cases each holding a gallon of spirits. Thames barges were similarly furnished, in fact it was said that there was hardly a craft from barque to dinghy which was not in one way or another modified to suit the requirements of the Trade; even the homely shrimping net often had its handle hollowed out to accommodate a long tin can containing twelve pints of the hard stuff. Even dog kennels were utilised; one washed ashore at Dungeness had a false roof concealing 30lbs of tobacco. Another method of illegally importing that commodity was to weave it up with strands of hemp to produce a substance virtually indistinguishable to a casual observer from ordinary rope; yet another ruse was to pack small amounts into oilskin bags and then coat them with clay—all the casual eye would see was a pile of innocent potatoes. 'A Dovorian of

Merchant Ships at the East India Company's Yard, Deptford (by Isaac Sailmaker 1721).

Hebraic origin' named Duffy was expert at disguising tubs under a skin of plaster of paris, studding them with gravel and shells and applying a final drape of seaweed. Brought in under cover of darkness and dropped just above the low-water line, as the tide receded they were left high and dry and indistinguishable from lumps of chalk, waiting for a harmless countryman clad in his gaberdine working smock (a garment also favoured by the smuggler) to come along the following morning with his horse and cart to pick them up and take them away for his legitimate trade of lime-burning — Dover to

England's first Line of Defence during the Napoleonic Wars. A Naval Squadron off the North Foreland. (Old print)

123

this day retains its Limekiln Street. According to a contemporary report,

> 'the scheme was so well thought out that it might have continued indefinitely, had it not been entrusted to a woman. One of the Dover smugglers passed the secret on to his sweetheart, who confided in another more favoured lover who happened to be an officer in the Coast Blockade.'

Even in those days, the Customs employed at least one 'sniffer' dog, although training methods have changed; from its early puppyhood the dog was accustomed to having all its meals laced with a liberal portion of spirits. After some months of this the practice was to starve him for a day and then take him out for a walk along the beach to search out his breakfast!

Sometimes, by sheer force of personality, the smuggler attracted royal attention, as did Richard Joy, known as the Kentish Samson, who demonstrated his prowess before William III. Once a drayman employed by the Ramsgate brewers Thomson and Wooton, he took to fishing and thence to the Trade at which he was caught and sentenced to death, which sentence was commuted to five years service in the Navy (see p.109). During his service on a man-of-war, so the story goes, the Captain overheard him demanding a double rum ration whereupon he was told that he could have this provided he satisfactorily demonstrated that he could do the work of two men. Forthwith he picked up a cannon off its carriage and carried it across the ship. It took six men to replace it and Joy was awarded his extra tot.

Although it was not strictly speaking smuggling, one individual hit upon an idea of cheating the revenue that was so ingenious it deserves mention. The fashion in ladies' hats in 1820s was for Leghorn bonnets, straw creations of magnificent proportions measuring three feet across. Made on the Continent, they found a ready market in England at three guineas apiece plus 50% import duty. Soon, a wily Dover

124

The Kentish Samson's grave,
St Peter's, Broadstairs.
(see p. 124)

The inscription
In Memory of Mr. Richard Joy
(called the Kentish Samson)
Who died May 18th 1742 aged 67.
Herculean Hero! Fam'd for strength
At last he's here, his breadth and length
See how the mighty man is fall'n
To Death the Weak and Strong are all one
And the same judgment do befall
God judges one, He judges all.

A popular thoroughfare for the Trade—*Snargate Street, Dover.*   (Old print)

milliner found and exploited a loophole in this regulation, for wearing apparel was exempt from duty when in use. He (or was it she?) proceeded to employ very cheaply

'a numerous company of women and girls of the poorest class to voyage daily from Dover to Calais and back, and also entered into a contract on most favourable terms with the steamer owners for season tickets for the whole band at cut rates. The sight of these women leaving town in the morning in the most deplorable headgear and returning in the evening gloriously arrayed as far as their heads were concerned was for some years a familiar and amusing one to the people of Dover.'

The Smuggler— A Sociological Phenomenon?

A sort of lewd people called Smuckellors, never heard of before the late disordered times, who make it their trade to steal and defraud His Majesty and His Customs.

(extract from a Parliamentary proclamation 9th August 1661)

Any self-respecting Kentish smuggler, were he acquainted with the concept of sociology, would have no doubt choked laughing on his 'flip'* at the title of this section, and yet the idea does merit serious consideration. Can the stereotyped images of blood and thunder, rum and baccy, silk, velvet, lace and gold be pushed aside to see the man beneath them? How

---

*A fiendish punch of rum, sugar, beer, gin and brandy, highly esteemed by all. A less fiery variant was 'hot' — mulled gin and beer.

126

Smuggling Fiction. R. Simpkin's idea of a Kentish smuggler. (see pp.72 and 131)

> 'Smuggler Bill stands six feet high
>   He has curling locks and a roving eye
> He has a tongue and he has a smile
>   Trained the female heart to beguile'.
>
>   (R. H. Barham, *Ingoldsby Legends*)

127

did he affect the community at large? What did his neighbours think of him? How did the writers and artists of his day see him and describe him? These questions apply to any county connected with the Trade, but the Kentish smuggler is as near as we shall get to the archetype. The effect of smuggling on the national economy was undeniably enormous; in one year (1784) the estimated consumption of tea was 13,000,000lbs with duty paid on less than half; similar situations obtained for spirits and tobacco. It was a much-used argument that smuggling provided extra pay for many a farm labourer who would otherwise have had a very thin time of it, as indeed he did once smuggling died out. Smuggling too, had far greater attractions than the more mundane rural tasks, as a writer in *The Gentleman's Magazine* (1753) pointed out: 'In several parts of Kent the farmers are obliged to raise wages and are yet distressed for want of hands to get in the harvest, which is attributed to the great numbers who employ themselves in smuggling along the coast.' The ensuing grain shortage made itself felt even in high places with the Royal Family renouncing all pastries and the Archbishop of Canterbury appealing to all good Christians to do likewise. The farm labourer's viewpoint may be well appreciated, seeing that one night's 'carrying' brought in as much as a week's or even a fortnight's honest toil and there was besides as much bread, cheese and beer as he wanted with the chance of a 10lb 'dollop' of tea thrown in; 'there was no harm in cheating Government, because Government often cheated you' was the usual reply to any charge of dishonesty.

The Vicar of Lynsted (a village between Faversham and Sittingbourne) had the courage to make his views plain:

'What we must complain of here is the monoply of land by the great farmers. If a little plot of a few acres is to be sold, they instantly have it, and if they have not money of their own, they are supplied by the County Banks, the consequence of which is, no butter, milk &c to be had. A labouring man in this county, having saved a few pounds, knows not what to do with it; he therefore too generally takes to smuggling, the consequence of which is soon very apparent; wickedness and its constant attendant insubordination and a disregard to the instruction of a Minister of Religion.'

It was, of course, the plain duty of the judiciary to condemn smuggling and to bring the weight of the law to bear upon those found guilty of 'the accurs'd thing'. Often their main shafts of condemnation were aimed at the organisers who were seldom arraigned before them; this was naturally scant comfort for the wretches shivering in the dock. In his

Smuggling Fact.
A Deal lugger beached at Dover (Artist and date not known).

summing-up at the trial of the Aldington gang at Maidstone (1827) Mr Justice Park made his feelings quite plain: 'If persons of the highest situation were not to purchase smuggled goods there would soon be an end to smuggling, but many persons labour under the delusion that defrauding the Revenue is no crime . . . ' It was at just that time, according to N. Williams *(Contraband Cargoes)* that the country was flooded with prohibited foreign silks: 'Fine quality French and Italian manufactures had always attracted the smuggler and the leisured ladies who flocked to the Continent never failed to bring home dress-lengths and lace . . . all the chief London stores dealt in smuggling wares . . . one West End store regularly obtained £200,000 worth of smuggled silks each year.'

Dr Samuel Johnson (1709-84) disapproved of the smuggler, defining him in his famous *Lexicon* as 'A wretch who in defiance of the laws of his country imports or exports goods without payment of customs.' Nothing if not fair, however, he balanced this with an equally jaundiced view of the Excise* — 'A hateful tax levied upon commodities and adjudged not by the common judges of property but by the wretches to whom excise is paid.'

Daniel Defoe (ca 1661-1731) was another who did not care much for the smuggler; passing through Faversham in 1724, he remarked upon its obvious prosperity due, or so he thought, to 'that wicked trade from Rumney Marsh.' Professor G. M. Trevelyan in *English Social History* takes a very different view, he states unequivocally that smuggling added interest to the life of the ordinary person almost as much as poaching did, and was regarded as equally innocent. Charles Lamb (1775-1834) the essayist was also on his side: 'I like a

---

*Customs were (and are) concerned with the taxation of imported goods, Excise dealt with home commodities e.g. the manufacture of Scotch whisky, and other forms of revenue such as the hated Window Tax. Division of responsibilities was not always clearly marked which led to rivalry especially at sea. The two departments amalgamated in 1909.

smuggler, he is the only honest thief;' he openly admires him for not cheating people but only the Revenue, an abstraction for which he cared very little, in common with many before and since.

Usually the fiction writers seem well disposed towards him; R. H. Barham (1788-1845), best remembered for his collection of grotesque stories *The Ingoldsby Legends* was for some years a Marsh parson who must have numbered many free-traders in his parishes of Warehorne and Snargate. He never condemned the practice, on the contrary, one of his characters, Smuggler Bill, although meeting a decidedly sticky end, was a most likeable person and especially attractive to the housewives of Thanet:

> 'There isn't a farmer's wife in the Isle
> But his eye and his tongue will wheedle her
> To have done with the grocer and make HIM
>   her tea-dealer.'

On the other hand, Bill's sworn enemy, the corpulent Riding Officer Gill, is made to look very foolish indeed.

Still within the realms of fiction, Dr Syn, the celebrated pirate turned parson and his jovial band of Dymchurch smugglers — churchwarden, sexton, choir and all — have been going strong now for nearly seventy years and fast heading for immortality. These characters who sprang from the fertile imagination of Russell Thorndyke (who is remembered to this day in the Marsh where members of his family still live) are said to have been founded on fact. James Finn mentions in his Journal (see p.23) a certain parson noted for his loquacity — 'he was a veritable Dr Syntax' who left instructions that he should be buried by the side of his coachman, a lifelong friend and servant. Is it too much to identify him as the original Dr Syn? Another pointer of some possible significance is mentioned by Keith Spence in *A Companion Guide to Kent and Sussex*: 'On the north wall of Snargate Church are two lead sheets dated 1700 taken from the roof, one of which shows that church repairers have been known to enjoy themselves. On it appears the names of the churchwarden, the plumber and *T. Apps, carpenter, and all his jolly men.* Nearby is a wall painting of a galleon in full sail . . . in 1743 the Revenue men seized a quantity of tobacco in the belfry and a cask of Hollands gin under the vestry table . . . ' Surely here are more pointers to the prototypes of Dr Syn and his smuggling gang?

Captain Marryat (see p.83) has many a smuggling scene in his adventure books and seems to be at his best describing action at sea, with the chase of the lugger across the stormy Channel being much more his forte than the smugglers' caves,

The *Smugglers Alarmed.*

(Old print)

the lonely inns and the riding officers much beloved by other writers of his period and style. His eye for detail in the rig and equipment of the craft he describes can never be faulted, which of course is only to be expected of an officer of the Royal Navy who had actually experienced that which he describes so well.

All said and done though, it cannot be claimed that the smuggler was universally popular, although he was nearly always tolerated. In the case of George Ransley (see p.59) for example, some, it is true, thought him *as fine a fellow as ever walked* but mainly because *he brought a lot of money into the place*; at the same time it is he who must shoulder the responsibility for the fact that *Aldington was a terrible bad place in those days, nobody decent liked to live there!*

Why, Polly, I hopes YOU ain't on the smuggling tack!
(Early Coast Guard)
(Old print)

Victorian readers certainly got good value from G. P. R. James (see p.15); he displays the golden age of Kentish smuggling with true melodramatic flair. At every opportunity, maidens shrink and tremble, wenches flaunt themselves boldly and villains behave in the truly base and vile manner expected of them. Every aspect of human nature may be encountered here; on the side of the angels, fighting for all that is good, true and beautiful one finds the gallant Dragoons major and landed gentleman Sir Edward Digby and, alongside him, his equally honourable chum and comrade in arms the Dragoon Captain Osborn; to support them in their campaign against the smugglers is a bearer of a good old East Kent name, the ruggedly trustworthy Riding Officer Mowle. Our heroine, the beautiful Zara, is surrounded by a host of minor worthies — squire, parson and magistrate — who are themselves attended by various subsidiary worthies, the statutory faithful old family retainers . . . The forces of evil are, it goes without saying, embodied in the local smuggling gang bosses, the unspeakable Old Ramley and his equally unsavoury son. Here is historical similarity to George Ransley who in real life was indeed assisted by his eldest son (who at the age of sixteen was entrusted with the accounts and correspondence and also led the carrying parties) but fact merges with fiction with the introduction of the affray at Goudhurst church which was fought by the Hawkhurst gang some fifty years before Ransley was born. Emphasising the fact that not every smuggler was an out and out villain past all redemption, Jack Harding, one of Ramley's men, has to meet a hero's death — or does he? Gentle reader, all will be revealed in the pages of *The Smuggler*. The stage, not to be outdone by the novelist, often depicted the smuggler; Samuel Arnold (1774-1852) featured him in an opera *The Smuggler's Cave* while Douglas Jerrold (1803-57) drew upon his experiences as a midshipman to give the late Georgian audiences at the Royal Surrey Theatre the enjoyment of his play *Black Eye'd Susan* relating the trials, tribulations and eventual triumph of Susan ('red and rosy as

Rigging out a Smuggler.
(Cartoon by T. Rowlandson.)   (Old print)

the King's head on the side of a fire-bucket') and her sweetheart, the honest and simple tar William. The chief villain was naturally a smuggler, the black-hearted Tom Hackett of Deal. (Where else?)

The free-trading way of life attracted the artist too; prints both plain and coloured, many of high quality workmanship, were turned out by the thousand to decorate the kitchen and parlour of the late Georgian and early Victorian era. Today they are highly regarded and keenly sought after. Some were by anonymous hands but there were also those of repute whose names are still familiar or even famous — Atkinson, Parker, Rowlandson, Willie, and even the great Turner himself, all essayed to portray the smuggler.

Henry Parker (1795-1873) was a Devon man, born and bred

Revenue officers attacking smugglers unloading contraband at Shakespeare Cliff, Dover. Artist and date not known. (Dover Library)

in a smuggling atmosphere. Travelling the country, he specialised in depicting the smuggler at work and so assiduous was he that he soon earned the title of 'Smuggler' Parker. Some of his Kentish scenes, published in the *Illustrated London News* are typical of his work; *The Smuggler's Cave* shows two craft unloading at Kingsgate and one of the men is most probably Joss Snelling (see p.45).

Parker's work is now most enthusiastically collected; perhaps not so popular but certainly well known in his day was Sir Francis Peter Bourgeois, RA (1756-1811). Mainly a society landscape painter, he lived and worked most of his life in London (his father was a rich Swiss emigré watch-maker) and he was possibly more at home at Court than on the beach. However, examples of his work are *Smugglers Attacked* and

Folkestone smugglers at work. (see p.139) (Turner)

Smugglers Defeated, both feature dragoons engaging smugglers against romantic backgrounds. Bourgeois was appointed painter to the king of Poland and received a knighthood from him, which he was permitted to use in England by special permission of George III. In later life, he founded the Dulwich College Picture Gallery; it was somewhat spitefully observed at the time that 'his own pictures are more than generously represented'. *(Dictionary of British 18th Century Painters* (Waterhouse 1981))

   Thirty years later, a much more eminent member of the Royal Academy evinced interest in the Trade. J. M. W. Turner himself, the Professor of Perspective, considered by most to be the greatest British water-colourist of all time, was very much his own man and determined to see and experience for himself everything before attempting its portrayal. This of course explains why he once had himself lashed to the mast of a steam-packet crossing the Channel in a blizzard — 'to transfer his feelings the better on to canvas'. His visit to Folkestone in 1821 resulted in the production of a set of watercolours showing smugglers at work; the detail and the atmosphere is so convincing that Turner who 'in his travels always mingled with humble and practical men' may well have been out with the gang. When the pictures are examined in order, a story emerges:

(i)   *Folkestone, from the sea* (original in British Museum)
      Here are tubs of contraband spirit being sunk at crack of dawn by a lugger flying the French tricolour, she being threatened by the approach of a Revenue cutter. Paying out the 'necklace' of tubs from the lugger is a six-oared rowing boat, a 'Folkestone cocktail' which will doubtless elude the preventive men in the very nick of time.

(ii) *Twilight—Smugglers off Folkestone fishing up smuggled gin* (original in a private collection in UK)
      The Revenue men have gone, lured away perhaps on a wild goose chase. The smugglers seize their chance to grapple up the sunken kegs; it is dangerous to leave them

too long for the salt sea creeps in to dilute the gin and convert it into a nauseous product known to the Trade as *stinkibus*.

(iii) *Folkestone, Kent* (original in Taft Museum, USA) (see p.137) The kegs are here being hidden again, this time on dry land. One man covers his face with an arm; has the digging tired him, or does he simply wish to remain anonymous? Perhaps both; Turner is noted for introducing these riddles, perhaps he wished to suggest both attitudes. In the background is 'Hurricane House' the ancient church of SS Mary & Eanswythe, so-called because of its exposed cliff-top position. Here rest together sailors, smugglers and preventive men, all strife forgotten.

(iv) *Coast from Folkestone Harbour to Dover* (original in Yale Center for British Arts, USA) Finally, we are shown that for once crime has not paid. A Revenue officer map in hand directs the recovery of hidden contraband.

An artist more noted for his military subjects, R. Simpkin lived at Herne Bay in the late 19th century. He did, however produce one set of ink-line drawings to illustrate *The Smuggler's Leap* (see p.142). Mr. Frank Gough of the Herne Bay Records Society, to whom I am indebted for permission to

Rochester Bridge. (Drawn by G. Shepherd, engraved by H. Adlard)

reproduce Simpkin's work, writes: 'As far as I know, they were never published . . . it is possible that they were drawn for reproduction as lantern slides to illustrate a local history lecture by his friend, Dr. Bowes, who recited the poem and brought in not only the drawings but appropriate photographic scenes . . . '

Alfred Sisley (1839-99) was born in Paris of English parents. Highly regarded as a French Impressionist, some authorities rank his work with that of Pissaro, Monet and even Renoir. He finds mention here not because he painted smugglers—he never did—but because his great-grandfather Francis Sisley (1748-1808) was a Romney Marsh smuggler 'whose capital laid the foundations of a respectable and prosperous family business dealing in silks and Paisley shawls'. Prosperous no doubt, but are there no reservations as to 'respectable'? At all events, the young Alfred was enabled, by his great-grandfather's efforts, to follow a safer and what was to him a more congenial way of life, living and dying in France, more French than English. Francis sleeps on with his family and alongside many another of the Trade in the leafy tranquility of Lydd churchyard with his descendants bearing his name in that town to this very day.

Scene of the rout of the notorious Hawkhurst gang by the villagers of Goudhurst 20th April, 1747. The gang was finally smashed in 1749—but smuggling went on much as before.

Down they went . . . over that terrible place . . . (R. H. Barham, *Ingoldsby Legends*)
Drawn by R. Simpkin. (see p.142)

And Still It Goes On . . .

> *On Saturday night a Customs cutter moored off the coast near Hythe spotted a dinghy which had crossed the Channel making its way towards the beach. As the two occupants were off-loading packages, Customs officers assisted by local police sprang an ambush . . .*

One might well imagine that this was a typical incident of the 1830s but in fact it is an extract from the *Daily Telegraph* dated 16th August 1982; latest statistics show that over four hundred Customs staff are employed on preventive duties in Kent alone. Besides the watch for the time-honoured commodities (tobacco still ranks favourite) a lookout must be kept for illicit drugs, livestock and pornography, added to which illegal immigrants and motor tax evasion have to be coped with; today, as of old, life and limb are sometimes

. . . which is called to this moment THE SMUGGLER'S LEAP! (see p.141)
(The Smuggler's Leap Caravan site, Acol)

risked — and lost — in the course of duty. Vanished long since, the spirit of the old free-trader must surely linger to chuckle over the nefarious activities of such as the two little old ladies who hit the headlines of the *Dover Express* (29th August 1980):

'Retired hospital matrons, they were the picture of respectability with nothing to declare. The Customs officers thought otherwise and their car was 'turned over' — an alcoholic's dream hoard was discovered. A 20 litre water container was full of gin; stacks of mineral water bottles were filled with gin or whisky. "Oh, aren't we naughty! We were up all night doing that job!" said one of the pair.'

The last word, however, must be allowed to our Victorian author, G. P. R. James:

'The nature of both man and woman, from the time of Adam and Eve down to the present day, has always been fond of forbidden fruit; and it mattered not a pin whether the goods were really better or worse, so that they were prohibited, men would risk their necks to get them.'

Four romantic views of smugglers.

A typical early 19th century Kentish smuggler.

An illustration for an article in the *European Magazine* on the Broadstairs smuggler, Joss Snelling, which was never published as it was feared that The Trade would have been glamorised. The building in the background is Farm Cottage, Snelling's home and the headquarters of his smugglers — the Callis Court gang. (see p.45)

145

Middle Street, Deal.
A well-known smuggling thoroughfare in 'that sad smuggling town'. (see p.21)

G.   R

TO BE SOLD BY AUCTION,

AT the Custom House, Deal, on TUESDAY, the 5th of September, 1826, at twelve o'clock at noon, precisely, the following GOODS, viz.—

3 Cashmere Shawls	1 Ivory Fancy Stick
4 East India Muslin Dresses	1 Pound of Camphor
13 yards East India Muslin	14 Sea-horse Teeth
1 Lacquered Card Case	1 Silver Box and Scraper
17 Pieces weighing 14 oz. 18 dwt. Gold Bracelets and Ornaments	1 Turquoise Necklace
	Ivory Fan and sundry Shells
3 Palampores	1 Coral Necklace & Bracelet
1 Ostrich Feather, Muff and Tippet	10 Cornelian Necklaces and Bracelets
63 Ostrich Feathers	115 Pieces India Ink
24 pieces of China-ware	20 Ounces Cajaputa Oil
3 Leopard Skins	28 yards Figured Satin
2 Tortoise-shell Snuff-boxes	2 China Gongs
	10 Bottles of Wine & Brandy

A fast sailing Lug-sail Boat, about 7 tons, in excellent condition—A Punt, called the Joseph of London—Two Boats in pieces, and sundry Boats Materials—Eight Anchors and Warps.

The Goods will be sold for Home Consumption, and may be viewed on the day preceding, and until noon on the day of sale. A deposit of £25. per Cent. on the purchase money will be required.

Contraband seized by the Customs was auctioned regularly to the public.

(Advertisement from Kentish Gazette)

147

Index

Illustrations are indicated by **bold** figures.